The
Inner
Work
of
Leaders

The Inner Work of Leaders

Leadership as a Habit of Mind

Barbara Mackoff
Gary Wenet

AMACOM
American Management Association

New York • Atlanta • Boston • Chicago • Kansas City • San Francisco • Washington, D. C.
Brussels • Mexico City • Tokyo • Toronto

This publication is designed to provide accurate and authoritative
information in regard to the subject matter covered. It is sold with
the understanding that the publisher is not engaged in rendering
legal, accounting, or other professional service. If legal advice or other
expert assistance is required, the services of a competent professional
person should be sought.

Library of Congress Cataloging-in-Publication Data

Mackoff, Barbara.
    The inner work of leaders : leadership as a habit of mind / Barbara Mackoff, Gary Wenet.
        p.   cm.
    Includes index.
    ISBN 0-8144-0590-8
    1. Leadership.   I. Wenet, Gary Alan.   II. Title.

HD57.7.M335 2000
658.4'092—dc21   00-038048

Printing number

10   9   8   7   6   5   4   3   2   1

Barbara Mackoff:

For my parents,
Sam and Selma Mackoff
and always,
for Hannah
and Jeremy

Gary Wenet:

This book is dedicated to my parents,
Sam and Eve Wenet.
*To my father, for showing me the deep fulfillment that comes in
helping to bring out the best in others.*
*And to my mother for teaching me that each person's story has
its own essential beauty—that each person's story is a story
deserving to be told.*

"The Water you touch in the river is the last of that which has passed and the first of that which is coming."

—Leonardo da Vinci
Notebook, Morals

Contents

Acknowledgments
Barbara Mackoff

I owe this book to conversations with sixty-five exceptional leaders. Writing a book to capture their candor, humor, and wisdom provided me with a singular and exciting challenge.

In understanding and mapping the inner work of these leaders, I was informed by lessons I have learned by teaching and consulting with many other remarkable leaders from around the world. Each of these leaders expanded my understanding of leadership as a habit of mind.

In exploring the legacy of leaders, I was grateful to be able to reflect upon Warren Bennis's stories of learning to lead, James Hillman's odes to individuality, James Kouzes descriptions of the leader within, and especially, Robert Kegan's brilliant illumination of adult development.

I have appreciated the involvement of Adrienne Hickey, our AMACOM editor, who immediately understood the power of this fresh paradigm of leadership. Her enthusiasm and responsiveness—coupled with her wonderfully pointed questions—guided the book to its final form.

I want to acknowledge the work of my colleague, Gary Wenet, who suggested that we explore the path to leadership, and provided some of the book's most compelling stories.

Special thanks to Darlene Cox, who cheerfully survived our fifth book together and prepared this manuscript in her usual flawless fashion. I am always grateful for her perspective and professionalism. And thank you to Ila McCullough for her careful preparation of the proposal and transcripts of the interviews.

I want to thank my mother, Selma Mackoff, the book's earliest reader, for being a vital source of support and insight. Special thanks to Jane Adams, for her wise consultation and to Diane Stein, Ken Muscatel, and Vivian Benjamin for their invaluable observations.

Finally, I am grateful to my daughter, Hannah, for the pleasure of her company at the day's end and the privilege of watching her leadership grow. And thank you, Jeremy, for your generous and gracious words and deeds at every turn of this project. Our discussions always enriched my sense of purpose.

Acknowledgments

Gary Wenet

As I reflected on turning fifty years old this past summer, I had a renewed appreciation for the rich personal and professional experiences that have shaped my life. I also came to realize that *The Inner Work of Leaders* project for me actually began when I was a young high school student. At that time, my counselor suggested that I interview our school psychologist to learn about the work that he did. That encounter would turn out to be a defining moment for me. I left the meeting with him that day inspired to become a psychologist. It was a decision that has given me the ongoing opportunity to help others develop their inner resources—to do the "inner work."

More than five years ago that I approached my colleague Barbara Mackoff with the idea of writing a book on leadership. At the time, I had been working with a client whose personal leadership style embraced the legacy of his father and reflected the lessons he had learned from him. My work with this client would become the seed for this book. My clients are a consistent source of inspiration and wisdom for me. I am full of respect for the commitment they bring with them for doing the inner work. I appreciate the collaborative nature of our relationship, and feel privileged to have the opportunity for ongoing learning that comes through our work.

I will always be grateful to the leaders who made themselves available to participate in this project. I left my interviews with each of them energized, with new perspectives for the book. Without their willingness to share very personal and heartfelt stories there would be no book—for their stories are the heart and soul of *The Inner Work of Leaders*. I want to extend my thanks for the depth of wisdom and experience that each of the leaders offered to this project.

So many individuals have been instrumental in shaping my career and the pathway that led to *The Inner Work of Leaders*. To my own exemplars along the way—Elizabeth McCandless, Alan Marlatt, Harold Mosak, Martha Perry, Arnold Katz, Steve Sulzbacher, and Johan Verhulst—my gratitude to each of you for the lessons and opportunities you offered me at different points in my life.

To my agent Elizabeth Kaplan, your wisdom and guidance has been invaluable. Thank you for your commitment to this project and to my own growth as an author. Your efforts went above and beyond in ensuring that this book found a good home. I will always be grateful for your ability to make me laugh at just the right moments. To my editor, Adrienne Hickey, I appreciate how enthusiastically you embraced this book and your belief in it representing a truly fresh perspective on leadership. Last, to the dedicated staff at AMACOM, thank you for your extensive efforts to bring this book to market in the best way possible and with its integrity intact.

I am truly blessed to have so many loving and supportive relationships in my life. To my family, friends, and colleagues who have been there with unyielding love and support along the way, my heartfelt thanks. To my three extraordinary children, who are giving shape to their own legacies—Sonia, with your dedication, tenacity, boundless energy, and enthusiasm—Simon, my wise little man, with your compassion, reflection, sense of fairness, and inventive nature—and Sophie, with your joyous spirit, determination, and infectious sense of humor—you are all a constant source of inspiration. Finally, to my wife, Andrea, the most exemplary leader I know. Your belief in me and this project has been a source of valuable energy at each step along the way. I feel fortunate to have a life partner who shares such enthusiasm for making dreams come true.

Introduction

The Inner Work of Leaders

F or more than a decade, we have been fascinated with the inner work of such leaders as Smith College President Ruth Simmons. Whenever we teach leadership seminars or conduct counseling and research interviews with leaders, we invite them to describe how they have created meaning, and learned from, the events and relationships of a lifetime.

It is fascinating to note how each leader translates the meaning into consistent thought patterns—*habits of mind*—to direct the way he or she thinks about, and reacts to, complex and challenging situations.[1] *Inner work* is our name for this process leaders use to leverage the lessons of past experiences to inform and invigorate their leadership.

When we talked to Dr. Ruth Simmons, we didn't ask her how she feels about being the first African-American woman to head a major college. Instead, we asked her to describe how she applies the lessons in leadership from the people and events in her life. Simmons offers a glimpse of how her mother influenced one of her convictions: the habit of mind of staying focused and committed to her work.

"People often ask me how I learned to be president of a college, and I tell them I learned to do it by going to work on Saturdays with my mother," says Simmons. "She was a domestic worker, and she let me follow her around while she was cleaning a house. When she ironed a collar she would say, 'Now, look, you have to fold the collar like this.' From her, I developed my own conviction about always doing work with great care and seeing every job through."

Ruth Simmons is one of the first of sixty-five leaders whose inner work we mapped for this book. Among them: a tribal chief

1

and a symphony conductor, the president of a baseball team and a brigadier general, an inner-city school principal and a Broadway director, a Fortune 100 CEO and a children's television producer, the director of a women's shelter and a U.S. senator.

Working with these exceptional leaders, we learned how far and long each leader carries the lessons learned from parents, teachers, and illuminating events. We began to polish a fresh paradigm: Leadership is not a role or a set of strategies. Instead, it is a *point of view* that begins with the inner work of integrating and translating past relationships and experiences into powerful habits of mind.

We also understood the *legacy* of leaders in a new way. Rather than defining legacy as what a leader leaves behind, we asked a trio of questions about how past experiences are transformed into a blueprint for a leader's point of view. We wondered, How do leaders absorb the impact of their families? How do they apply lessons from defining experiences and people of influence? How do they integrate life-changing circumstances and events?

These three aspects of legacy—the family template, the world as teacher, and the moments of meaning—are the starting point for the inner work of leaders. And while each of our leaders has a unique legacy, they are all remarkably alike in their ability to translate their experiences and relationships into one or more of the five following inner thought patterns, which they found central to their success as leaders:

- *Reflection:* the capacity to examine and appraise their own behavior and impact on others
- *Framework:* the strategy of interpreting negative events with a resilient inner narrative and response
- *Attunement:* the practice of setting aside assumptions, reversing roles, and learning from every person in the organization
- *Conviction:* the ability to trust, value, and speak from their own experience
- *Replenishment:* the craft of counterpoint, that is, restoring perspective and renewing resources

All of the leaders offer distinct—and often whip smart, funny, and tender—ways they have translated their legacy into these five habits of mind. From these leaders, we learn how it feels to be in charge and how they count their habits of mind among their most precious assets.

The leaders' examples invite you to mobilize your own legacy as a leader. Because every person leads a team of one. Only when you do this inner work and understand the people and experiences that have influenced you can you develop a point of view for leading and inspiring others.

The Inner Work of Leaders is not a how-to book about becoming a leader. We provide, instead, the opportunity to study examples of leaders whose strategies and styles are defined by their capacity to learn from their life experiences. As you glimpse the inner work of these leaders, you can apply their examples and explore how creative you have been (or can be) in transforming your legacy into rich habits of mind in your leadership.

This book is for people who are in charge of an organization and for those who want to be. We hope that each of you will recognize your experiences in learning to lead. Whether you are a leader or a leader-to-be, this book demonstrates how to draw upon your life's rich legacy and to turn the challenges in your work into opportunities for leadership.

The Legacy of Leaders: Finishing the Story

Broadway and film director Daniel Sullivan (*The Heidi Chronicles; I'm Not Rappaport; The Sisters Rosensweig; Dinner with Friends*) offers a wonderful image of the legacy of leaders. He says, "My father owned a movie theater, and at age 12, I began to work as an usher. My parents would take me to the theater at 6:30, when the box office opened; the show would begin at 7:00; and I would be taken home at 7:30. I saw the first half-hour of everything, but I never saw the end of those movies. So I would construct the endings in my own head. I always had to finish the story. I was often disappointed when

I would see the films later and find an unfamiliar—and not particularly good—ending." Sullivan adds, "When you direct, you tell the story your way. I wanted to gain control of the story."

Like Sullivan, each leader we encountered offers rich recollections of life experiences. They recall the details of family, the role of teachers, and illuminating moments as the legacy from which they learned essential lessons about leadership. And, like Sullivan, each example from their legacy is the beginning of the story rather than the end. Each experience or encounter offers them an opportunity to "finish the story."

In part 1, The Legacy of Leaders, as you explore the legacy of dozens of intriguing leaders, you can consider the three following aspects of your life story. They comprise a legacy that only you can "finish writing" by transforming your experiences into resources for leadership.

The Family Template: How Leaders Transform the Influence of Their Families

As a young girl, Cathleen Black, the former publisher of *USA Today* and current president of the Hearst magazine empire, spent many hours talking to her father about his food manufacturing business. She was fifteen years old and her father was fifty when he lost his eyesight. Black remembers, "I watched the way he handled his physical disappointments and challenges, how he was driven by positive ambition and refused to let a quirk of fate stop him."

Cathleen Black's relationship with her father created a *template* for her leadership—a pattern for developing her own inner resources. Her father's example led her to cultivate a habit of mind called *framework:* the ability to explain and label negative events in a positive light.

Black explains how her father's resilient thoughts helped prepare her to tackle the discrimination and controversy she encountered as a founding member of *Ms.* magazine in the 1970s. "I learned how to keep dodging bullets and refused to take no for an answer," she says.

Our research reveals how leaders translate the lessons learned in their families and use them to craft the habits of mind that guide their leadership. With each leader's description of his or her family template, examine how you draw upon the lessons learned from your family.

The World as Teacher: Exemplars and Experiences

Costco CEO Jim Sinegal was an eighteen-year-old college student when retail legend Sol Price—founder of The Price Club—became his boss at FedMart. For Sinegal, Sol Price became an *exemplar*—a model for the habit of mind of conviction.

"Sol was the brightest and most honest person I ever met," says Sinegal. "He was passionate about the business, recognized talent, and was quick to hand out the credit to someone else."

Sinegal still remembers a meeting, more than thirty years ago, that conveyed Price's conviction about giving credit where credit is due: "When I worked at FedMart, there was one manager who was obsessed with taking the credit and quick to blame when things went bad. But Sol saw through him. To teach us all a lesson, Sol used a weekly meeting to purposely raise hell about something that was wrong in one of the stores. I wondered why he did it. But when he saw that this manager let two of his employees take the blame, he fired him within a week."

The legacy of Sol Price's convictions is apparent in Sinegal's point of view about being in the spotlight. "It's improper for one person to take credit when it takes so many people to build a successful organization," says Sinegal. "When you try to be top dog, you don't create loyalty. If you can't give credit (and take blame), you will drown in your inability to inspire."

Many leaders describe how the world outside of their families offers them two kinds of models: exemplars (like Sol Price), who offer models of behavior, and guiding metaphors, or the images that create models to define experience. In reading their stories, you can reflect on the teaching models that have mobilized your leadership.

The Moments of Meaning: How Leaders Create Clarity about Events

On autumn Sunday afternoons, 130 million people watch National Football League President and COO Neil Austrian do his job. "You can't go anywhere," notes Austrian, "where someone doesn't have an opinion about something you are doing wrong." Austrian recalls a moment of meaning that ripened his conviction and shaped his legacy as a leader who relies on his inner authority and values the authority of the people he leads.

Austrian was twenty-eight years old, working at Laird Investments, and about to close a deal to buy a company, when he began to have second thoughts about the company's manager. As Austrian remembers, "The CEO at Laird told me, 'I'm going to trust your instincts; you've lived with the guy for the last year. If you don't want to do the deal, we won't do it.' "

Austrian completed the buyout, but he replaced the manager two years later and harvested a rich lesson about relying on his inner authority. He explains this moment of meaning: "At twenty-eight years old, I took the easy way out. But I filed it away in my brain, to try not to make the same mistake again. I should have trusted my instincts."

This conviction became a habit of mind for Austrian, who now draws upon the lesson he learned by giving his managers and employees the latitude to strengthen their own inner authority. "I don't micromanage," he says. "If someone wants to go off and do something he thinks is right and he is passionate about it, I am willing to trust his judgment—even if I have more experience."

Like Austrian, leaders create clarity about events by recalling these *moments of meaning*—the life-changing events—that have shaped the development of their habits of mind as a leader.

Habits of Mind: Returning to the Music

To glimpse a habit of mind in action, imagine that you are listening to a magnificent performance of Vivaldi's *Four Seasons* conducted by the concertmaster/first violinist. Then, when the violinist is in the middle of a demanding solo, the unthinkable happens: A string breaks with an inelegant twang. The audience gasps and falls silent.[2] But what if the concertmaster smiled, shrugged, reached over to borrow the second violinist's instrument, and returned to the music?

This musical moment defines a habit of mind with great economy. It is an inner resource that allows you to develop a point of view to confront successfully the pressure, demands, and decisions of leadership and "return to the music." The leaders we studied and worked with have demonstrated five distinct habits of mind that we will detail further in part 2. These inner resources enable them to develop a consistent point of view, one that defines and enriches their experience of being in charge.

Reflection: How Leaders Examine Their Experiences

Gerard Schwarz, celebrated music director of the Seattle Symphony, the New York Chamber Symphony, and beginning in 2001 the Royal Liverpool Philharmonic reflected on his first meeting with his mentor, the great composer and conductor Leonard Bernstein. He details a vital lesson learned about the importance of cooperation, not competition, in leading an orchestra.

At the time, Schwarz was a trumpet player in his first rehearsal with the New York Philharmonic Orchestra. Several minutes into the first piece of music, Bernstein stopped the orchestra and boomed, "*Who* is the brilliant new trumpet player?" He greatly embarrassed—and isolated—the new musician on the block.

Schwarz shares his insight about the rehearsal, and his ability to learn from his experience illustrates the result of reflection as a habit of mind. He maintains, "I learned many things from Leonard Bernstein; but on that day I saw how dangerous it can be to single out a musician for praise at the expense of the rest of the orchestra. To this day I don't feel competitive, even with other conductors, because we have the same purpose. And I can't imagine taking too much credit for the success of my orchestra. I think about my musicians, my board, my development director; we are all here because we love music."

The habit of mind of reflection allows leaders to find meaning and learn vital lessons from their experiences. Through their examples, you can also apply the tool of reflection to study your actions and create a context for your leadership.

Framework: How Leaders Interpret Negative Events

In her twelve terms in the U.S. Congress, Patricia Schroeder's ability to frame negative events with humor earned her many a sound bite on the nightly news.[3] It was Schroeder who called Ronald Reagan "the Teflon president" and who presented Speaker of the House Newt Gingrich with a mock Oscar—for best performance by a child actor—for his public petulance about his seat on *Air Force One.* Describing the nine years of her nonstop lobbying to pass the Family and Medical Leave Act, Schroeder compares her life to the Bill Murray movie *Groundhog Day.*

"You did the same thing over and over again," Schroeder says. "You passed family leave and the Women's Health Initiative and, then, the president vetoed them, and you couldn't get enough votes to override him. Then you came back next year and reintroduced the bills, and got your cosponsors, and went through the whole thing again."

Schroeder's framework, or her explanatory style, is a habit of mind that allowed her to label and interpret this battle so that she remained a resilient leader until the bill's final passage. "My mother always told me there are people who wring their hands and people who roll up their sleeves," says Schroeder. "Being a history major, I understood that the first time ideas were brought up they don't go. You have to stay in for the long haul, keep educating people, and finally get them to move. So we just kept dusting off the bill and bringing it back."

Exceptional leaders use the habit of mind of framework to label, explain, and interpret frustrating or negative events. From their examples, you can learn to interpret your own challenges with resilient habits of mind.

Attunement: How Leaders Understand (and Learn from) People They Lead

As president of the University of Michigan in the 1980s and president of Princeton University in the 1990s, Dr. Harold Shapiro might have become rather nonplussed about student protests. Yet what he learned in coping with those protests, ranging from civil rights to divestiture in South Africa, offers a heartfelt description of his habit of mind of attunement. Shapiro is a leader engaged in the act of finding meaning by attempting to understand the views of the protesters who have occupied his office over the years.

As Shapiro explains, "Whether these people are doing the right thing or the wrong thing in protesting (or interfering with your day) is not the point. What really matters is for me to care enough to ask myself, 'Is there something here I should be understanding?' When people arouse themselves to project an idea they may be naive, mistaken, outrageous, and full of hyperbole. So I try to push that aside and say, 'How can I give some meaning to this?' Unless you try to engage the experience and make some meaning of it, it goes away."

Shapiro remembers one scene from a shouting match at the University of Michigan: "A group of students were yelling at the well-meaning regents and calling them murderers and Nazis. I said to myself, 'These are young people; to them, everything is a holocaust. But these are not just people who are having a good time on a Thursday afternoon. They are trying to say something.' "

Shapiro invited them to come into his office so he could "figure out what they were thinking." The students did change Shapiro's mind. "Not that my thoughts were similar to theirs," he says, "but in listening, I had a new and better view of what was at stake here and what the university's response ought to be."

Leaders like Shapiro, who draw upon attunement to understand and respect the people they lead, suggest how this habit of mind deepens your connection to the people you lead.

Conviction: How Leaders Express the Value of Their Experience

George Lynn, president and CEO of New Jersey's AtlanticCare, recalls how his first job interview with John Rich, the owner of a nonprofit agency in Atlanta, fostered his convictions as a leader. At the time, Lynn was desperate. He remembers, "It was the beginning of summer; my wife, Pat, was pregnant; the company I had worked for had gone out of business; and I was literally without a job or money." When Rich offered Lynn the job and asked if he could start in September, Lynn responded, "By September, we will have starved to death."

Rich was shocked by Lynn's situation and by the idea that a leader would close down a company without providing a rainy day fund for his or her employees. Rich promptly put Lynn on the payroll. "In retrospect, it was great business," says Lynn. "He just acted on his values; he wasn't looking for anything in return. But what he got was a loyal employee. I worked hard for that man."

John Rich's influence is clear in the way George Lynn shapes his convictions about job security at AtlanticCare. More than once, he has battled his board to avoid company layoffs. As he explains, "I see our employees troubled by the downsizing of hospitals across the country. We can't expect to improve the level of quality when people feel such a personal threat. So we are working on a company-wide contract to answer the question, What is it that keeps senior management from guaranteeing that every person will have some kind of job?"

A focus on the habit of mind of conviction creates a blueprint of how leaders express consistent values, purpose, and inner authority in their day-to-day decisions and actions.

Replenishment: How Leaders Restore Their Perspective

Harry Kamen, chairman of the board and CEO of Metropolitan Life Insurance Company, was twelve years old when he attended his first opera, Verdi's *Don Pasquale*, at the Metropolitan Opera House in

New York City. "My uncle tipped the usher to move our seats out from behind a pillar so we could see," recalls Kamen. Fast forward to fifty years later, Kamen met with opera legend and director of Lincoln Center Beverly Sills and agreed that MetLife would underwrite the $4.5 million Public Broadcasting Service series *Live from Lincoln Center*—a telecast seen by up to 4 million people.

Kamen's alliance with the arts is both professional and personal. His experience with music illustrates the habit of mind of replenishment. "Although I am not very emotional on the exterior," says Kamen, "sometimes the first few notes of a Mozart or Schubert quartet can bring tears to my eyes. I find this experience of music clears the mind and psyche and gets me ready for the next day."

Kamen finds replenishment in the athletic as well as the artistic. He jokes, "There's no better relief of a day's tension than getting in a little white room with another person and hitting a little black ball as hard as you can against the wall." And he restores his perspective as a leader by choosing activities "completely different from my work": attending suppers at the Museum of Natural History or sitting on the board of Smith College and New York mayor Rudolph Giuliani's Advisory Council.

The closing chapter of this book considers the paradox of replenishment as a habit of mind: how a leader's outer actions can become a source of inner strength. You can apply these examples of replenishment to restore your perspective, recharge intellectual capital, and reinvigorate your commitment to leading.

Leaders on the Couch

"No one has ever asked me these questions before," said Barnes & Noble CEO Leonard Riggio when we asked him about the isolation he felt as a young leader. "I never get asked about this," noted Senator Paul Wellstone of Minnesota of the lesson he learned as a professor at Carlton College when he was fired for community activism and then was rehired. "Are you trying to put me on the couch?" demanded the top executive of a real estate empire, declining our request for an interview because he "didn't want to be psychoanalyzed."

Admittedly, some details of the inner work of leaders seem to be classic couch material. For example: One media mogul describes working near his parents as "Samson getting a haircut" and a transportation czar reveals he had spent his childhood crisscrossing the country to visit his divorced parents and years later, becomes a top executive of both a major airline and railroad.

The premise of *The Inner Work of Leaders* is that the emotional lives of leaders is cumulative. We explore how relationships and events from the past are translating the present point of view of leaders. But rather than browsing a Freudian Web site, we intend these explanations to be architectonic—not psychoanalytic. Because in listening to leaders, we discovered the layering of experience and meaning that provides a foundation of inner strength in their leadership. This approach owes more to Marcel Proust than to Sigmund Freud. In each leader's remembrance of the past, they transform their legacy to create vibrant habits of mind in the present.

Instead of a couch, this book offers you both a window and a mirror in learning to lead. First, the leaders' life stories provide a window for viewing and understanding the life legacy that has shaped each leader's distinctive strengths. Next, as you consider the experiences of these compelling leaders, use each story as a mirror to reflect deeper truths about your own potential as a leader.

We underline our intention by describing the difference in two leaders' responses to a similar situation. Several years ago, at a black-tie holiday dinner we sat with ARCO chairman and CEO Harold Sorgenti. While other ARCO executives danced by our table, Sorgenti bitterly recounted a story about a letter, which he keeps in his desk, from a teacher who told him he would never succeed. Clearly, Sorgenti relished rising above his teacher's expectations. Yet thirty years after receiving the letter, Sorgenti offered this self-portrait: "I don't get stressed; I *give* stress."

We were reminded of Sorgenti's still-angry response to his teacher's discouraging words when we interviewed Time, Inc., President Bruce Hallett. With wry humor, Hallett recalled a similar experience. A high school Latin teacher at Exeter once informed Hallett he "wasn't going to make it," greeted him with "I see you are still here," and then apologized to him on graduation day. Thirty years later, Hallett is a leader who describes himself as a "teacher" and "coach."

We are not suggesting that Sorgenti's scarlet letter shaped his entire sensibility as a leader or that the grace note of a graduation-day apology determined Hallett's good-natured recollection. Still, the contrast of these two leaders underlines the book's central idea: Leadership is less a role or set of strategies and more a point of view. It is a viewpoint that results from creating meaning, and learning from, the events and relationships of a leader's lifetime.

This definition of the inner work of leaders was summed up by the scientist and novelist Aldous Huxley.[4] "Experience is not what happens to you," noted Huxley. "It is what you *do* with what happens to you."

Part One
The Legacy of Leaders

Chapter 1

The Family Template

Transforming the Influence of Family

"I t is not that I was born in a log cabin, but close to it. I came from a position of no money and no power," says Al Gamper, the president and CEO of the CIT Financial Group, when describing how the legacy of his family shaped his leadership. To trace Gamper's family template, we asked several leading questions: What did you learn from your parents as leaders of the family? How would you describe your role in the family? Was there a circumstance or event that touched every family member?

Al Gamper explains how his family life became a template—both a gauge and a pattern—for developing the habit of mind of conviction about corporate equity. "My family background made me aware that society shouldn't be so class conscious. Because of my father's economic struggles, I try to run CIT with an equity in how people are treated—where there is equality of purpose and people can differentiate themselves in their performance. I work to eliminate class and racial distinctions and trappings of the hierarchy. The employees in the mailroom call me Al."

Descriptions of the family template of numerous leaders reveal their family experiences as imprints that cast both shadows and light in their earliest education as leaders. Like Al Gamper, each leader adapts lessons learned from parents as leaders and in response to family events and circumstance.

A Family Template

Al Gamper was a sophomore at Rutgers University when his father's chronic emphysema forced him to quit his job. Gamper assumed the role of provider and dropped out of school to support his parents and older brother. He took a job at Manufacturer's Hanover Bank in Manhattan and finished his last two years of college in four years of night school. For Gamper, his family circumstance created a lifelong conviction about job security.

As he explains, "I watched my father going broke, paying bills. He didn't have the umbrella of an organization to help. As president of CIT, I am very aware of benefits that relate directly to families. We started the CIT Foundation to help employees in trouble. With its funds, we have sent terminally ill children to camp, helped divorced mothers pay their mortgages, and covered the costs of a funeral. Umbrellas are important here. We do these things because I've pushed it, because of what I went through as a kid."

Gamper offers another example of how his family history had been translated into company policy. A consultant once came in and suggested that the CIT Financial Group could save money by dropping all of its retirement programs. "God, I really took that personally," says Gamper. "Why? Because my own background made me so aware of security and treating people well. I want to build an organization that stays strong with good benefits and demanding high levels of work."

It is intriguing to note that Gamper also calls CIT a "paternalistic" company. Clearly Gamper's assumption of his father's role of provider became a pattern for his convictions as a leader. Yet his father's chronic illness did not lessen his influence. Consider how his father's leadership of the family offered Gamper an unforgettable lesson in equity and diversity. As Gamper explains, "My father had a big impact on how I treat people. He was an early advocate of diversity. No biases or bigotry were vested in me."

Gamper remembers a moment of meaning that took place when he was ten years old and called a schoolmate "a nigger" at the dinner table: "My father, who was a strict Swiss, glared at me and asked, 'What did you say?' And I said, 'You know, a nigger.' Then he said, 'If I ever hear you use that word in this family, I will never talk to you again.' And for a couple of days after that, I wondered if I was still a Gamper. If he would have hit me with a stick, I would have felt better. Instead, I was treated like a pariah by this man I really admired. I never used that term again."

Years later, we can still see the link between his father's demand for tolerance and Gamper's own conviction about avoiding the trappings of race and class distinctions at the CIT Financial Group. Gamper also uses the bully pulpit of his leadership to embellish his father's message of tolerance. As the honoree at the annual meeting of the National Conference of Christians and Jews, he retold the story of his father's lesson in leadership and shared his own meaning: "We are all so conscious of racial issues. We have programs and associations working at it. But what we need is better parents. If you all had parents like mine, we wouldn't have as many race crimes in America."

Defining the Template

Gamper explained, "I'm a big believer that your environment and family life in your first ten years on this planet have a big impact on how you think in later life. You don't think about it consciously, but when someone asks me, 'Why do you think that is so important?' some of these incidents come back." Gamper's comment echoed the advice of another leader who decried class distinctions. Karl Marx suggested that evolution might be studied in reverse with an eye fixed on the evolved species while looking backward for hints.[1]

In this light, Papa Gamper's supper-time threat can be viewed as a "hint" that spoiled his son's appetite for racial slurs. Yet Al Gamper's expression of conviction and the actions of the CIT Financial Group to promote equity have evolved as his own invention. The family template is a powerful influence on leaders. Still, as psychologist James Hillman suggests, children are not simply the effect of parental causes.[2] To understand this distinction requires a more precise definition of the family template.

A template is a gauge, mold, or pattern that functions as a guide to the form being made. It is also a way of organizing information on a computer screen. The early family life of leaders like Al Gamper suggests how brilliantly leaders organize the information of family patterns and experiences and transform them into habits of mind that define their leadership.

Al Gamper organized two aspects of the family template—the lessons learned from a parent's leadership and from the family's economic circumstances—and used them as a guide in his evolution as a leader. This inner work integrated lessons from the past to create the habit of mind of conviction in his leadership. Gamper's conviction is a habit of mind that leads directly to his strategic actions—from creating a culture at the CIT Financial Group that embraces equity and job security to advocating racial tolerance and diversity in the business community.

Parents as Leaders

The evolution of leaders "in reverse" can be clearly mapped by observing Al Gamper's convictions in the corporate arena and by examining the work of two intriguing leaders of nonprofit organizations: Doug Wheeler, the principal of Zion Preparatory Academy in Seattle, a school that welcomes children primarily from African American and lower-income families who have been overlooked in other school settings; and Beckie Masaki, the executive director of the Asian Women's Shelter, a facility in San Francisco that offers sanctuary for victims of domestic violence. We found their parents' leadership was vital in crafting their inner resources as leaders.

Doug Wheeler, Principal of Zion Preparatory Academy: The Conviction of Family

Principal Douglas Wheeler calls Seattle's Zion Preparatory Academy "the Thirty-second Avenue Miracle." This inner-city school began in 1982 with six students, one teacher, a budget of thirteen dollars, and books taken out of dumpsters at nearby public schools.[3] By 2000, Zion had grown to 534 students and moved into a $7.4 million facility that is financed by corporate and community support.

The imprint, or the hint, of Wheeler's parents as leaders is apparent in this scene from a Zion Prep schoolroom. Mark, a teacher, asks the students what is different about Zion Prep. The list begins: The students wear uniforms, lunch is free, and there is no gym or video games. Mark persists, "What else?" One of the students explains, "Because we call you guys 'Brother' and 'Sister' instead of 'Mister' and 'Missus.' " When Brother Mark asks, "Why do we do that?" the student answers, "Because you love us." Then Mark says, "And when you love each other, what are you?" The class shouts, "A family!"

In Doug Wheeler's conviction about family at Zion Prep is the legacy of a powerful lesson in leadership taught by both of his parents. Wheeler talks about his pride in watching his father, a probation officer, walk down the street when he came from work: "This was the 1950s. He was the only Negro on our block who wore a suit and carried a briefcase," Wheeler says. And his father always came home to a full house. At one time, there were sixteen children—biological, adopted, and foster kids—in the Wheeler household.

The high census of children was his mother's idea. Wheeler says that every Christmas or holiday his mother brought a new baby home for a visit from the hospital where she worked, and the baby never left. He recalls his mother as a leader: "Mama was the disciplinarian. She was always on our backs. But she taught me how to give, how to embrace children and take care of them."

He remembers one particular Christmas when his mother brought home his future brother Gordy, "a two-week-old baby who was weak and unable to eat." Because her husband had told her, "Woman, no more children," Mama Wheeler asked six-year-old Doug to be her accomplice and hide the baby upstairs when his father got home. Predictably, Gordy squawked and was discovered by Dad, who demanded that he be returned to the hospital the next day. Instead, here is what Wheeler saw: "At three o'clock that night, I came downstairs and found my dad sitting in the living room, singing to Gordy and trying to get him to eat. He stayed up all night trying to feed that baby who became my brother."

Three years later, Wheeler's father taught him another unforgettable lesson in family values. Wheeler describes this moment of meaning: "When you sit at the breakfast table with sixteen kids, cereal doesn't go very far. One morning, when I reached for the little bit of cereal that was left, one of the other kids reached for it too. I got mad and said, 'Give me that cereal! You are not one of the real children.' " His father took Doug upstairs, spanked him, and lectured, "You understand one thing: We are *all* family, and they are all your brothers and sisters." Wheeler was a quick study. He recounts, "By the time I came downstairs and looked around the table again, I knew that I would never say that to any child or anybody again."

To visit Zion Prep is to understand how far Wheeler has carried his father's sermon about the cereal. As he explains, "The thing that makes this school different is that we are willing to be a family for that child. We are willing to be Mom, Pop, Uncle, or Grandpa— whatever it takes to fit into a child's life so they realize that there is a family here."

In this school-as-family, Wheeler wants children to experience unconditional love. His message is, "You can mess up. There will be discipline and consequences, but we are still going to love you." Wheeler takes every opportunity to let the children know how valuable they are, telling them, "There is never going to be anyone like you." Just like his father, Wheeler believes that when you tell children how valuable they are, they will treat other people that way. "That's why we call each other 'Brother' and 'Sister,' " says Wheeler. "That's what I got at home."

Wheeler has transformed the commitment and tenderness of his parents as family leaders into a habit of mind of conviction that guides his leadership at Zion. Wheeler hopes to pass on these lessons in leadership to another generation of leaders in his role as principal. "When I look at all my children here, they are all my brothers and sisters," he says. "As the oldest, it is my responsibility to lead each one of those children, because each one of them is somebody's mom or dad in the future."

Beckie Masaki, Executive Director, Asian Women's Shelter: Balancing Community and Self-Reliance

Beckie Masaki, executive director of the Asian Women's Shelter in San Francisco, was raised in a house on Tenth Street in the heart of Sacramento's Japanese American neighborhood. Her family's fish market, the unofficial clubhouse for the community, was on the same block. Masaki proved to be an astute observer of her parents' leadership at work and at home, recalling her parents' conviction about their community as well as their lessons about relying on one's inner authority.

After ten years of working in the field of domestic violence, Masaki was convinced that other available shelters couldn't meet the needs of Asian women.[4] When she opened the Asian Women's Shelter, she explained, "For Asian women, safety is about interdependence and having a community that is going to help you." And Masaki is clear about the source of her conviction.

She recalls, "My parents' store was like a community center. When elderly people came in to cash their Social Security checks, my brother drove them home. If someone was sick, we brought them rice. My father would give people jobs and secretly loan them money. People would just hang out here. I see my work as an extension of that sense of community. It's too bad that feeling of neighborhood is destroyed in this country, because that's what I try to re-create and rebuild in a new way at the Asian Women's Shelter."

For Masaki, the family's sense of community also became a template of trust. She remembers her brother complaining about the way her father ran the store. "My brother would accuse the egg man of shortchanging us, but my father would never count," says Masaki. "He'd say, 'We have been doing business with his family for years. We should trust them. It is more important to have the relationship than to argue about a few eggs.' "

Her family's conviction about community takes a different form in Masaki's own emphasis on collaboration. "We put a high value on working with other groups. You have to invest in the relationship and keep an eye on the big picture of the relationship itself. Being angry about the small points can do a lot to destroy trust," she says. Like her father, Masaki trusts people to bring their best to the table.

Yet why did Masaki, who had come from such a loving family, choose to take charge of a shelter for battered women? Because she has translated her family legacy of community in her own terms. "I have the privilege of not having been hurt, so it is my job to be part of the solution," she explains. "All of us, whether we have experienced domestic violence or not, need to be part of the solution. It may not be happening to me as an individual, but because it is part of the community I belong to, I experience it just as deeply as if it were happening to me."

At the Asian Women's Shelter, Masaki draws upon the resource of her conviction about community. She also understands how her mother's model of inner authority has influenced the core convictions of the shelter's treatment program. She says, "A lot of my philosophy about the shelter comes from my mother's philosophy of empowerment."

Masaki offered the following snapshot of her mother's strategy for teaching her to rely on her own strength and authority: "I never saw my mother cry. She was fiercely independent, competent—the opposite of a victim. If I would cry, my mother would be compassionate while giving me the message. You have to be tougher. If I was in trouble, I could run to her and it would be a safe place."

At these times, Masaki's mother would tell her, "I can see that you are in pain, and I will take care of you. But you need to learn to do this yourself." It is fascinating to note at the shelter how Masaki has integrated her mother's tough love into a model for ending the cycle of domestic violence.

She details her approach: "The first time someone comes in, we validate the fact that she has been hurt. She needs someone to nurture her and believe her story, to understand that she has been in a violent and dangerous situation. We offer her rest and food. Then comes the empowerment part. We tell a woman, 'You have a lot of strength, and we are giving you a safe place so you can recover that strength within yourself.' If someone asks me whether she should get a divorce, I tell her, 'You are the one who knows best.'"

By translating the legacy from her mother in her own words, Masaki reminds each woman that she has the tools and authority within herself to make her own decisions.

Like Mother, Like Daughter

Al Gamper's father was a teacher of tolerance, and Doug Wheeler's mother wrote the book on extended family. Beckie Masaki also has learned powerful lessons in leadership from her parents and defined her leadership by integrating the information and patterns of her family template in a fresh and moving way.

Throughout our interviews, we discovered leaders who have translated admirable lessons from their parents' leadership in their own terms. Yet this positive influence is not the only way that the family template creates a pattern for leadership. We also encountered leaders whose parents' behavior suggests caution or correction rather than inspiration.

Parents as Negative Models: Danger and Opportunity

For some leaders, parents became what one executive called "anti-role models." Whether parents are leaders who evoke caution or inspiration, they become catalysts for the growth of inner resources. Consider the example of Barbara Davis Blum, chairman and CEO of Adams National Bank (the largest women-owned bank in the United States). She does not mince words in describing her mother's influence and her desire to become a boss who was not like her mother.

"My mother was the anti-role model," says Blum. "She was a housewife with little education, few interests or friends, who got a migraine whenever confronted with a problem. I looked at her and I thought, 'If I don't do something with myself, make sure I get the best education, and develop some leadership skills, I could be just like my mother.'"

The impact of parents as negative models can be compared to the word *crisis* in Chinese calligraphy. In the Chinese language, the word *crisis* is drawn with two distinct characters. One means danger; the other, opportunity. Similarly, for exceptional leaders, even a negative lesson—a crisis—can become an opportunity to evolve. The experiences of John Mackey, founder and CEO of Whole Foods, who turned the crisis of his father's criticism into an opportunity to develop the resource of reflection, illustrate this point.

John Mackey, Founder and CEO, Whole Foods: The Opportunity for Reflection

When John Mackey became a teenage vegetarian, his parents didn't want him to join them for dinner. Today, Mackey is the CEO of Whole Foods, America's largest chain of natural foods supermarkets.[5] While he credits his father's leadership and support as essential in building his economic literacy as a leader, his father's short fuse for failure sent Mackey on an extended search for an alternative role model. Mackey's experience demonstrates how even a negative parent model of leadership can foster the growth of inner resources, such as, in Mackey's case, a habit of mind of reflection.

Mackey remembers, "My dad was the kind of guy that if I brought home a report card with all As and one B, he wouldn't say, 'That's great!' He would say, 'Why did you get the B?' He was a very successful businessman, and even though I had some early successes, my father was incredibly judgmental and had little tolerance for failure." His father's impatience, says Mackey, contributed to a crisis in confidence—one in which John dropped out of college six times and didn't regain his confidence until he started a business at age 24.

Mackey, who has been called the "accidental grocer," is a mindful leader who sought to learn from his experiences by studying religion, philosophy, and spirituality both in and out of college. In the early years of Whole Foods, his search for meaning led to his involvement in a program called "the Course of Miracles," a spiritual philosophy created by two psychologists. In this program, he found a model of reflecting and learned from the experience of his father's intolerance for failure.

As he explains, " 'The Course of Miracles' is a pathway about forgiveness, about people making mistakes. I learned that forgiveness comes into play in overlooking people's mistakes. Instead of judging and finding fault—like my father did—we can let mistakes become lessons." Reflecting on his experience in leading Whole Foods, Mackey admits, "One of the reasons Whole Foods practices forgiveness is that I started this business at [age] 24 and made more mistakes than anyone. Yet these mistakes also meant that I had been open to new ideas."

Mackey has created a unique corporate culture based on what he has learned. At Whole Foods, the team, rather than the hierarchy, is the defining unit. Teams can make decisions without getting the green light from upper management. Mackey also practices what he calls "no secrets management," where every team member has access to all of the operating and financial data from corporate headquarters in Austin. The result, according to Mackey, is that "in most companies, people take a risk and if something goes wrong, they get their heads chopped off. Here, because we are decentralized, we let people take a lot of risks and let mistakes be lessons. We don't have a lot of rules handed down from Austin. We have lots of self-examination going on."

Mackey's unique response to failure, and his encouragement of reflection, is apparent in his description of an employee on his third round as a store team leader. Mackey says, "His first two times he didn't do a good job, and we had to pull him out of that position. In many companies, he would just get fired, but we recycled him into other jobs, and he learned the lessons and applied for store team leader again. The second time, he did a better job, but not good enough. So we moved him out again. Now, the third time, he's back in that position and doing an outstanding job. He's one of the best team leaders in the company."

John Mackey's inner work has allowed him to travel a great distance from the dangers of his father's reaction to failure. And it helped him transform a family template of intolerance to create the opportunity for a companywide resource of reflection.

Circumstantial Evidence: What Leaders Do with What Happens to Them

Parents' leadership is central to the legacy and inner work of leaders. Yet in almost every interview, leaders also described family events and circumstances that stimulated the growth of their inner resources. For example: Philadelphia mayor Ed Rendell's beloved father died when Rendell was twelve years old; Senator Paul Wellstone was ten years old when his older brother was hospitalized for a mental breakdown; and CEO John Bryan of Sara Lee was given one of his father's companies to run when he was the ripe old age of twenty-four.

The aspect of "circumstance" in creating the family template recalls Huxley's definition of inner work. The key in each leader's life was not what happened to that person, but what he or she did with what happened. The route to leadership was directed by how each leader made sense of family events.

To understand this point, consider two leaders from two dramatically different circumstances: Gene Silberberg, the president of Bigsby & Kruthers, the premier menswear retailer in Chicago, and Bruce Hallett, president of Time, Inc., the publisher of *Time* magazine. For both of these leaders, family circumstances offered a lesson in developing the habit of mind of framework—one that stimulated their resilient, optimistic interpretations of challenges in their leadership.

Gene Silberberg, President, Bigsby & Kruthers: Choosing a Habit of Mind

During the 1990 presidential debates, President George Bush wore two ties given to him by Gene Silberberg, CEO of Bigsby & Kruthers, a Chicago menswear store that counts Michael Jordan and

Dennis Rodman among its frequent buyers. "Our customers buy suits, but we are in the entertainment business, looking for the last little exclamation point," says Silberberg about the seven Bigsby & Kruthers stores that have wet bars, large-screen televisions, and humidor-equipped cigar-smoking lounges.[6] The festive atmosphere of the stores is a stark contrast to Silberberg's remembrance of his childhood circumstances.

Both of Silberberg's parents were Holocaust survivors; they met and married in a relocation camp. His father had been a successful businessman in Austria who had lost his lumber export business in the war. He later emigrated to Chicago, where he could only find work as a laborer. He left his last paycheck—fifty-six dollars for a week's work—in a dresser drawer and committed suicide when Silberberg was eleven. As Silberberg recalls, "I grew up hearing, 'Your father is sick because of the war.' I was raised in an atmosphere where you were taught to always be looking over your shoulder. I not only had to live my own life, but I also had to live the lives of people who had died. I had to carry a double pack."

In spite of this burden of circumstance, Gene Silberberg is a resilient leader, one who transformed his parents' pessimism into a habit of mind of framework. He has interpreted the horror of the Holocaust and created a more optimistic style in his life and work.

"There are two kinds of people who came out of the Holocaust," he explains. "Some had seen the worst that could be done between men and had walked away with hopelessness. They had seen the darkest side, they would always look through dim and distrusting glasses, they would never really see the light again. My parents were like that: dim and grim."

Yet Silberberg was stimulated to seek the alternative. "On the other side, I saw people who were liberated, who felt like birds soaring above the earth. They had lived through the worst and God said they were to live, and they feel a responsibility to live life to the fullest." Clearly, Silberberg has decided to soar. Yet his family circumstances remain a part of his equation.

For Silberberg, once you make the decision to come out of the fire, you have little to lose. "So you take risks and you revel in the risks. You don't fear loss because everything is fleeting. The feeling of being on borrowed time gives you confidence," he says. "But that other part is always biting at your tush. It keeps you running smarter and a little faster."

Silberberg needs his optimistic framework in this era, when the menswear business is experiencing a record slump. Mention "casual Fridays" to Silberberg, and he tells you about the daunting challenge facing his company: "Right now, it's the biggest struggle we have ever had. The customer who has been wearing suits his entire adult life is switching to casual sportswear."

Still, he interprets the challenge of his customers with his resilient point of view: "On paper, I shouldn't even be here." But Silberberg takes the long view, because he can remember a time when he couldn't get a loan from Lake Shore Bank without an army of cosigners. Today, the former site of that bank is his newest Michigan Avenue store. "I'm still here," says Silberberg. "I'm taking the last suit wearers and trying to please them."

As he leads his company to counter the "jeaning" of corporate America, Silberberg wonders, "Will the tide turn before we do?" His deeds and words reveal his optimistic framework. He wonders, "Can I compete with the casual look sold by the Gap and Banana Republic? I have to try to outwit them and outwork them and out-create them. I have to keep asking, 'What is the atmosphere of my stores? How will we advertise?'" His conclusion: "The only way to find out is to take it on."

Consider, now, a second tale of the role of family circumstance in the evolution of framework.

Bruce Hallett, President, Time, Inc.: Over-the-Top Optimism

When asked how his employees at Time, Inc. would describe his strengths as a leader, Bruce Hallett answers with the speed of light, "I think they would say my abiding characteristic is my sense of optimism, my belief that we can get somewhere different than we are today. Maybe it is an over-the-top optimism, but it's something people seem to pick up on. They say, 'If he thinks we can get there, damn it, then maybe we can!' "

When asked to consider his past as the prologue for this optimistic framework, Hallett's response is equally swift. "I'd have to go back to the model of my mother," he says and proceeds to describe a defining childhood event when he cut off two of his fingertips in his mother's meat grinder. This memory, Hallett says, is still "as clear as riding the train this morning."

"The meat grinder was one of those newfangled 1950s gadgets," Hallett remembers. "My mother was using it to cut up a leftover roast. I pushed the garbage can over, climbed up next to her, and asked if I could help. She handed me a wooden spoon, and I remember thinking, 'Why do I need a spoon if Mom's not using one?' The minute she turned her back, I stuck a piece of roast into the grinder and sliced off the tops of two of my fingers."

After the accident, Hallett was hospitalized for several weeks. Here, his mother showed him a model for framing, or interpreting, the traumatic event. Instead of talking about the details of the accident, she insisted on a more resilient and optimistic interpretation. In the weeks and years after the accident, she always focused on how her son had brought Christmas cheer to the other patients in the hospital.

"Once I was bandaged up, I was just this happy little kid with this goofy little hand," said Hallett. "So whenever she told the story, my mother would remind me of how the doctors had carried me around the hospital to do their rounds and that I had been a great source of joy to everyone in the hospital. And she insisted on her interpretation, repeating this story again and again. She would tell me that I had not been in pain; I was just happily being myself. There was no 'poor Bruce.' Instead, she offered the idea that I had done some good, that the accident was not a tragedy or a setback."

Hallett calls this framework typical of his mother. "Throughout my life she told me, 'If you strike out, you will get a hit next time.' She taught, modeled, and lived in a resilient way," he says. In another example, Hallett remembers bringing home a note from a teacher complaining about his handwriting. He lamented then,

"Look Mom, I've got these two shitty little fingers. How can I possibly write as well as the next guy?" But Mother knew best. "Don't you ever let that be an excuse for your performance," she warned. "I never did," recalls Hallett, noting, however, that even her resilient framework couldn't help him throw a curve ball. "I just couldn't get the last flick of spin," he jokes.

The circumstances of a childhood accident created an opportunity for Hallett's mother to model her optimistic framework. Many years later, Hallett continues to communicate a similar habit of mind in his leadership. He offers the example of his tenure as chief of *Time*'s Australia bureau, when he presided over the less-than-stellar launch of *Who Weekly,* the Australian version of *People* magazine. Both sales and ad revenues had been disappointing, but instead of despairing, Hallett framed the situation as temporary. He explains, "First editions are never a vivid reflection of what the magazine will be."

Because of his resilient framework—which resulted in his interpretation of the disappointing launch—Hallett was able to rally his troops at the next editorial meeting. He talked about the importance of what they were doing and of his personal commitment to the magazine for the long haul. "It was a defining moment for the magazine," he says. "People really understood that I would be, as they say in Australia, the last guy off the boat."

Reflecting on the lesson he learned, the meeting was also a defining moment for Hallett as a leader: "In that meeting, I understood that leadership is not about imitating somebody else, but about being yourself. The things that worked best for me—my enthusiasm, optimism, and energy—were the biggest resources I had as a leader. I realized that playing on those resources was the best chance I had for being successful."

Avoiding the Traps of the Family Template

Family life offers lessons in leadership in a variety of ways: by seed sentences that grow in meaning, by sermon, by model and example, through inspiration and caution, in life-changing events and circumstances. Each of the scenarios described here illustrates how the medium of family life sends clear messages about how to, or how not to, behave as a leader. But only the leaders-to-be who are watching and listening receive those messages.

Exceptional leaders share the willingness and ability to create a new meaning from their family experiences. They transform their family template into a model for powerful habits of mind that shape their point of view and strategies as leaders. Yet there are two traps in tracing the family template.

The first trap is determinism. A view of family as destiny ignores the cognitive and emotional gifts—and the wonderful quirkiness in temperament and personality—of each individual leader. Countless leaders grew up in families with economic strife. But how many of them have translated the experience into the supportive corporate culture Al Gamper leads at the CIT Financial Group?

We have little desire to join the noisy discussions about nature versus nurture. Nor do we want to join in the furor du jour suggesting that parents don't matter, but genes and peers do.[7] Instead, the family template is best understood in terms of medieval chemistry and the art of alchemy. In alchemy, a combination of elements creates a new, distinct (and even more valuable) element. Similarly, the study of the inner work of leaders reveals the leader and his or her family were combining elements that together created rich inner resources.

A second trap lies in ignoring the power of continuing education. Our consulting and training work has shown us that every leader-in-waiting can be taught to draw upon the legacy of family. The ability to translate a life legacy into habits of mind is a leadership strategy that can be learned and practiced.

Former Congresswoman Patricia Schroeder and PC Connection cofounder and CEO Patricia Gallup have both combined and transformed the legacy of family into rich habits of mind.

Former Congresswoman Patricia Schroeder, President, Association of American Publishers: The Anchor of Conviction

By the time former Congresswoman Patricia Schroeder was five years old, her family had moved so many times that Schroeder would advertise her new-kid status by placing her toys on the curb and then sit in a nearby chair to try to lure new friends. "We were like tumbleweeds," remembers Schroeder, whose pilot father was called in to teach in the U.S. Army Air Corps and forced to close his private airport in Oregon after the 1941 bombing of Pearl Harbor.

Schroeder's family circumstance, along with her parents' leadership, contributed to her capacity to rely on her own conviction. Clearly, Schroeder is the daughter of parents who declared their own (and her) independence. Schroeder offered a portrait of her working mother: a teacher in an era where women ironed sheets and wore white gloves when they went over to someone's house (so they could test for dust).

"Mother didn't buy into that," Schroeder says. "The lesson she taught me was that it was better to learn to play the piano than to make sure it is dust-free. She taught me to do what you think is important and ask yourself, 'Am I making progress in what is important to me?'"

About her father's legacy in her leadership, Schroeder explains that her father's baby sister was a tomboy who could outrun and outshoot her brothers. "So my father didn't think I needed to wear pink organdy and sit on silk cushions," says Schroeder. "He allowed me to take flying lessons and to get my pilot's license when I was sixteen. It was fun to be able to do those adult things. I was proud to be different—to have achieved something besides having the best tan."

Then there is the matter of Schroeder's allowance. In 1948, her parents scandalized the second grade when they began to give her an allowance of thirty-five dollars a month, from which she would have to pay for the bus, lunch, school supplies, and Tootsie Rolls. Schroeder shares the meaning of these lessons about trusting her own authority: "From day one, they conveyed tremendous trust in me. I lead the same way today: I run my own office horizontally; I drive my own car, dial my own phone. I don't hover and lecture. I give people a job and trust them to do it. I think that is one of the reasons we kept winning the Best Congressional Staff of the Year Award."

Schroeder's years in Congress are marked by this ripening of her inner authority, such as her willingness to stake out and stand by often unpopular, lonely convictions. As she explains, "I came from Colorado, from Marlboro country, and I chose to work on the issues of women in the military, family and medical leave acts, and gun control. But I'm comfortable enough to form my opinion; I'm not about to defer. The more someone tries to intimidate me, the more I think they don't have the facts."

When Schroeder describes these steadfast positions, she reveals she has transformed her mother's model of defining what is important. Schroeder delivers this message with her signature humor and candor: "Leadership isn't something you put on, like a dress," says Schroeder. "You can't just take polls every day. You have to know what matters to you, and stay in there and educate, and let people know what you are about."

Schroeder is clear about the sources of her conviction. "It comes from the trust my parents put in me." Her inner work—how she has transformed this template of trust—is apparent in her definition of politics. As she explains, "Politics is easy. I'm not an actress; I never tried to hide my positions. I figure anyone who voted for me knows I am pro-choice, anti-gun, and pro-working women. I still got elected. If they didn't like my positions, they could elect someone else."

Patricia Gallup, Cofounder and CEO, PC Connection: The Habit of Attunement

Patricia Gallup, cofounder and CEO of PC Connection, the nation's largest mail-order and catalog personal computer company, described how her family's "dinner theater" had developed her habit of mind of attunement. Gallup's father—a carpenter, union organizer, and mediator—would direct Patricia and her sister in role play to imagine and debate different sides of an issue. Picking a topic in the news, such as civil rights or the Vietnam War, he invited his daughters to view the issue from all angles.

At other times, Gallup's father would bring his work home. She recalls, "Sometimes at dinner he would talk about grievance cases he was working on and ask us to imagine the point of view of both the employee and the manager. He would challenge us to ask why each person felt so strongly—and to think about a possible positive outcome for both people."

Gallup sums up the impact of this family practice of attunement: "I think it was good for my sister and me to be exposed to thinking about issues, putting ourselves in the other person's shoes, and trying to understand their point of view." Gallup calls attunement "the basis of everything I do as a leader."

As she explains, "Whenever I am making a decision about the company—whether it has to do with customers, employees, or vendors—I ask myself, 'What would they be looking for? What are their expectations? How can I make a decision that is in the best interest of all parties?' I try to take everyone's viewpoint into account. If I don't have time to talk to them, I can try to consider the situation from what their point of view might be. If I do a good job of this, I can make a decision that everyone will buy into."

For Gallup, understanding and going beyond customers' expectations is the reason for PC Connection's reputation as an innovator in customer service and support. Case in point: PC Connection doesn't rely on marketing studies to assess customer needs. "By the exercise of putting ourselves in our customers' shoes," says Gallup, "we can be intuitive about people's needs."

Gallup's exercise of attunement inspired the design of two key customer innovations that have become industry standards: PC Connection was the first company to offer toll-free technical support before, during, and after the initial sale. "I could empathize with the needs of new PC users," says Gallup. "When we started this service, the industry was new; there were a lot of new products. Because computers were so new, we felt our customers needed that additional help and feeling of security when deciding who to buy from."

A second customer innovation—shipping every order overnight—was the result of Gallup and business partner David Hall's ability to envision their customers. Gallup observes, "In this global business environment, people have a different sense of time. We could imagine our customers working late in the evening to get information pulled together for the next day. We didn't want them to wonder, 'Is the company open?' We want them to know that we are open seven days a week, twenty-four hours a day, and if they order by 2:45 A.M., they will receive their order the next day."

Gallup's passion for being attuned to the needs of customers—what she calls "exceeding their expectations"—can also be traced to her family template. She recalls how her mother, a registered nurse, would volunteer to care for sick neighbors, and her father worked as a volunteer firefighter: "My parents were living on limited resources. Yet they were always reaching out to others, often going beyond other people's ideas about what another person would do for you."

Gallup was eight years old when her father fought a neighbor's house fire until dawn. She remembers, "When he came home, he had trouble breathing and his hands began to blister. It turns out he had stood so close to the fire and inhaled so much warm air, that his lungs had burned and scarred."

Whether Gallup is responding to customer needs by offering overnight delivery or responding to employee needs by developing affordable housing near PC Connection's first corporate headquarters in rural New Hampshire, she sees the influence of her parents' attunement. Gallup sums up this lesson in leadership: "I think my parents' commitment—the whole idea of treating people right—is the source of my passion for the customer and doing the right thing for them."

Why All Leaders Are Alike

When we interviewed Leonard Riggio, CEO of Barnes & Noble, he was tired of reading about his family template. He explains, "A lot has been written about my dad and how he was a great prize fighter who instilled fear in his opponents. Reporters find it convenient to dismiss what I have done by playing on that, as though I'm just some kind of tough guy or bully knocking off the competitors." Riggio deconstructs his dad in a very different way: He sees him as a ringleader and a teacher, not a fighter.

Len Riggio set the record straight, talking about his father's empathy, energy, and innovative ideas: "My dad was a boxer, but what people don't know is that he abhorred violence. He would walk out of a John Wayne movie and say, 'Those people are not heroes.' He picked more people off the canvas than he put down on it. His whole life was about inspiring people to become more than they thought they could be."

When Riggio wants to inspire his staff and to excite them "to think outside of the box," he talks to them about admiring his father's ahead-of-his-time ideas. As he explains, "My father was always coming into my office with ideas that later made someone else a fortune. I remember how we scoffed at his idea of starting takeout Italian food at our neighborhood restaurant. Now it is a thousand-store chain."

Riggio's lesson from his father's leadership lies in the habit of mind of attunement—being open to new ideas from everyone. As he puts it, "I realized how often we are dismissive of people who are bright and creative. We put them in a category and say they can't sit at the table. My father's farsightedness showed me how important it is to embrace ideas from everyone."

Listening to Riggio, we are tempted to tinker with the novelist Tolstoy's wisdom about the family template. This magnificent storyteller has suggested "all happy families are alike." Our observation is that all exceptional leaders are alike because they create a rich meaning from their family template.

For these leaders, the family's past is prologue, and they finish the story in the development of their habits of mind. Yet family is only part of the story. Because it takes more than family to educate a leader.

NOTEBOOK: THE FAMILY TEMPLATE

CIT Financial Group CEO Al Gamper translates the experience of his family's economic struggles into his conviction about creating an equity of people and purpose at his company.

- Describe a family circumstance, event, milestone, or loss that touched every member of your family. How did this experience contribute to your perspective as a leader?

- Specify a family member whose convictions have influenced your leadership. Identify the ways you have translated their values in your own terms.

Time, Inc. President Bruce Hallett suggests that his mother's resilient response to a childhood injury inspired his positive framework as a leader. For Bigsby & Kruthers President Gene Silberberg, his parents' pessimism was a cautionary tale he rewrote in his optimistic habit of mind.

- Identify someone in your family who offered a model of explaining or interpreting negative events. Compare and contrast your approach to framing challenging events with this early example.

For CEO Pat Gallup of PC Connection, the role playing during family dinners created a template of attunement. By drawing upon this capacity to value the customers' experiences and put herself in their shoes, she created key customer innovations at PC Connection.

- Describe a family member who offered an example, a seed sentence, or sermon about the importance of understanding and valuing each person's point of view. Or describe a family member who conveyed a lack of regard.

- How do you (or can you) apply the lesson of these examples in your leadership?

Recall Al Gamper's statement: "I'm a big believer that your environment and family life in your first ten years on this planet have a big impact on how you think in later life."

- Interpret this statement in terms of how the lessons from your family have influenced the way you think about leading your organization.

Chapter 2

The World as Teacher
Learning from Exemplars and Experience

When Esther Torres, founder of the Community Development Corporation, made up the guest list for the ground breaking of the Margarita Mendez Apartments for emancipated foster youth in East Los Angeles, she included former Goldman Sachs general manager Rich Atlas. "I met Rich 20 years ago—when I was a student at UCLA—and we have stayed in touch." Explains Torres, "Even though we talk infrequently, he has been an inspiration. He is part of me; he is in my heart."

Torres continues, "I was in a MBA program, a young whipper-snapper who wanted to go into investment banking. After Atlas spoke at a graduate seminar, I called him and told him, 'I want to do what you do.'" Atlas met with Torres, introduced her to several colleagues in the field, and then challenged her: "Esther, this is a tough business; it will knock you down and stomp on you. What makes you think you have what it takes to be an investment banker?"

"The first thing that came to my mind was the farm," remembers Torres. "I told him, 'I grew up on a farm, and I'm from several generations of farmers. And there are some years when you can have a storm and it wipes you out completely; but you don't turn your back and walk away. What it does is bring you together even more. You stick to it and make it work.'"

Atlas then recommended Esther Torres for an internship with Salomon Brothers in New York. He told her, "You are going to New York. You tell the people at Salomon Brothers about that farm."

Esther Torres illustrates how much the world outside of the family teaches leaders by introducing people and experiences that become models for developing their habits of mind as leaders. The leaders we met have allowed us to look beyond the clichéd connection between leaders and role models.

So rather than rounding up the usual suspects, we describe the two kinds of models that contribute to the legacy of leaders: the *exemplars* (like Rich Atlas), who offer models of behavior, and the *guiding metaphors* (the farm), which create models to define experience.

Esther Torres describes how the metaphor of farming provides a model for her day-to-day experiences as a leader. Her inner work lies in translating the images of farming into the habits of mind of framework and attunement.

The Framework of Farming: "Keep Your Eye on the End of the Matter"

Sixty years ago, Esther Torres's grandfather packed the family into an ancient Model-T and traveled over the mountains to settle in the San Joaquin Valley. Intent on leaving the troubled neighborhoods of East Los Angeles (L.A.) behind, he started work as a ranch hand. Although he was unable to read, write, or speak English, he eventually became one of the biggest farmers and landowners in the valley. Three generations later, when Esther Torres returned to East L.A., she intended to tackle some of the problems that caused her grandfather to travel north. To meet the challenge, she brings the framework of farming to work every day.

As director of the Community Development Corporation, Torres cultivates an optimistic habit of mind that she links directly to farming. As she puts it, "The central message of farming is for us to work together to deliver a performance. So you must keep your eye on the end of the matter to produce the wheat, cotton, or corn that is going to benefit the whole picture. Whether I am in the classroom with a student or negotiating with the federal government, it is the same feeling: We are going to do it together for the end of the matter."

At the Community Development Corporation, "the end of the matter" is producing self-sufficiency in a population of eighteen- to twenty-year-old former foster youth—a population officials say has a 50 percent chance of ending up on the street within six months of coming of age. This goal is accomplished in the award-winning H.O.M.E. program.

In the program, many of these young adults become involved in revitalizing dilapidated housing in Los Angeles County. Resident youths in programs like the Margarita Mendez Apartments learn the skills needed to rehabilitate and sell single-family homes, from entry-level construction skills and landscaping to real estate marketing.

Torres draws upon the framework of farming to encourage her staff to create optimistic interpretations of frustrating, challenging events. She says, "Every day we try to reiterate the end of the matter, because you never know what the day is going to bring. We have to remind ourselves that even though the day-to-day is difficult, we must keep in mind that it goes to a much bigger picture, and the end of the matter (the result of our program) is going to be good."

Focusing on the end of the matter has taught Torres to approach failures and mistakes as opportunities for learning. As she explains, "On the farm there are physical indicators that things don't work: The plant dies, the cotton doesn't grow. You can work with your heart and soul, and the season wipes you out completely. You don't unravel and wonder, Was it worth it? You ask, What is the lesson here? What can we do together so our time will be more productive? Where would we like to be in five years? And what are the avenues we can take to get there?"

Torres relied on this optimistic habit of mind to sustain her during the depressed real estate market in the early 1990s. During that time, she drew upon another metaphor gleaned from farming: opening up channels. This powerful image of opening new channels inspired the creation of the Community Development Corporation and nurtured Torres's resource of attunement.

Opening up the Channels: A Model of Optimism and Attunement

In the early 1990s, Torres had left investment banking and was working as a real estate developer to revitalize housing in South

Central Los Angeles. "We were in South Central before it was fashionable," Torres explained. Then, after the riots, everybody focused on that area. Suddenly, our sources of funding began to dry up as HUD—a major network supplying homes to us—went into the market. We had to change our approach to this business and to South Central L.A."

She approached this business downturn with her usual optimistic framework. She recalls, "We looked at the end of the matter and asked, Where do we want to be in five to six years? And what are the channels we can take to get there?" Once again farming provided the framework. "When you are a farmer, unless you channel the flow of water to flow through the rows to nurture the trees or crops, they are not going to grow, and they are not going to bear fruit. You've got to channel that water. There could be water everywhere, but if it doesn't go to the right place, you don't have a crop," says Torres.

She also applied this metaphor to guide the reorganizing of her company. Torres says, "You can always open up new channels. Instead of throwing up your hands if it doesn't rain, you can ask, 'What new channel can I bring to nurture this crop?' "

Torres opened the channel of community. Traveling to different community centers in Los Angeles County and listening to the people's needs helped Torres formulate a plan to transform the structure of her business into the nonprofit Community Development Corporation. Its mission is to meet the needs of former foster care youth who would participate in the rehabilitation of housing in South Central and East L.A. These refurnished homes would also open up home ownership opportunities for low-income families or first-time home buyers.

To accomplish the goal—and to nurture her crop—Torres opened up channels of communication between two county agencies that had never worked together. Partnering the Community Development Commission and the L.A. County Department of Children's Services, Torres's new nonprofit company created the H.O.M.E. program.

Clearly, Torres has translated the experience of farming into a model and framework of optimistic problem solving. Torres's definition of her leadership is also guided by the metaphor of creating channels. "As a leader, that's what I do; I channel energy," she says. Clearly, she has also expressed the image of channels into her habit of mind of attunement.

Whether working with first-time home buyers in the Hispanic community, or teaching a class at the Margarita Mendez Apartments, she opens up channels for growth. Of her interest in homeless youth, she says, "They haven't had a voice. We have lost them, lost their energy. No one has benefited from that energy. The government says we are contributing to them, but I see how we can get that energy and channel it."

To underscore her point, she tells us about a bright young man at the Margarita Mendez Apartments. She describes him as "smart enough to have become a successful criminal." Instead, he is enrolled in a college engineering program, and Torres plans to make him a supervisor for her rehabilitated housing developments throughout Los Angeles County.

Listen to Torres's attunement and respect for this young man's potential: "I see him going from having no focus and no goals to creating a life plan. His energy has been channeled to help him understand that as a leader he can be very effective. He is a good example of someone whose energies have been channeled not only in his life, but for the good of people who will cross his path. We will all benefit from him."

Metaphor: A Model to Define Experience

Esther Torres emphasizes that Rich Atlas, a Goldman Sachs general manager, recognized her potential for leadership in her spirited telling of her "farm story." Here, two parallel ideas are at work. First, Rich Atlas is a classic exemplar—a role model of leadership behavior. His attunement to Torres's strengths helped channel her energy into sound career planning. Years later, Torres translated the model in her own terms by recognizing the potential of homeless youth at the Margarita Mendez Apartments.

But foremost, Esther Torres's own resources of attunement and framework were the result of the farm's curriculum. In each example, the guiding metaphor of the farm has become a model for defining her experience as a leader. Whether she is keeping her staff focused "on the end of the matter" or opening "new channels" to create community alliances and release the energy of homeless youth, Torres returns to the metaphor of the farm.

The logic of Aristotle illuminates how leaders like Torres use metaphors to create meaning and resources in their leadership. As Aristotle explained in the ancient Greek best-seller *Poetics*, metaphors allow us to see similarity in the dissimilar and to create a connection between previously unconnected things.[1] In the same way, Torres uses her guiding metaphor of the farm to connect the lessons she learned from farming with her day-to-day experience of being in charge.

The world of the farm was a great teacher for Torres—the kind of teacher who brought out the best in her. The guiding metaphors of leaders like Torres are one powerful way leaders leverage lessons from their legacy into habits of mind in their leadership.

Two dramatically different examples underline this point. Seattle's superintendent of schools, John Stanford, is a leader who draws upon the guiding metaphor of the military to enrich his resources of self-reliance and framework. And Tim Girvin, CEO of Tim Girvin Design, relies on the Zen metaphor of ch'i to create the attunement that guides his decisions, from choosing the furnishings in his corporate offices to designing the title credits for Clint Eastwood's film *The Unforgiven*.

John Stanford, Superintendent of Seattle Public Schools: The Military as Metaphor

In the countless press profiles of Superintendent John Stanford of Seattle, most articles refer to him as a "former army general." When Stanford—who had never held a position in education—was offered the job, pundits found the military metaphor irresistible and often asked, How will a former general lead the teaching troops?

In recalling his legacy, John Stanford offered a detailed description of the military as teacher that moved far beyond the glib guess of the press. He explained how the military became a guiding metaphor in his leadership, one that provided a model for directing his experiences of being in charge. Clearly, he had leveraged the lessons of military service into the habits of mind of conviction and framework.

For Stanford, his military experience offered a metaphor and model of taking responsibility for the actions of his troops. As a twenty-three-year-old second lieutenant, Stanford was first assigned to command a company in Germany with 125,000-gallon tankers. Over the years, he was responsible for a company in Vietnam; a battalion of 1,500 people in Fort Hood, Texas; for 3,000 people in the Republic of Korea; and served as a major general under General Colin Powell in the Persian Gulf War.

Reflecting on these leadership experiences in the military, Stanford describes a metaphor that guides his leadership of Seattle's schools: "I learned that the United States Army has some very strong values. It is not a leadership trait to say, 'Oh, it's not my fault. The lieutenant did it, or the private did it.' "

Here, Stanford is describing a shouldering responsibility, which is central to his habit of mind of conviction. "If something goes wrong under your leadership, it is your fault. You never hold your people responsible. If you had wanted a different outcome, then you should have done a better job in instructing them," he says.

For Stanford, employee failure is the result of not ensuring that the policies, procedures, values, and mission were more clearly understood. Yet when he talks about his policy toward school principals, he outlines the delicate balance of shouldering responsibility with encouraging his principals to share the responsibility for their schools: "Once something goes wrong in their schools, I will step in front of it and take the heat—get the backlash from the news—so they can get on with their work."

But behind closed doors, Stanford talks to his principals about what he calls "unrecoverables," or the failures of responsibility that are grounds for dismissal. Among them are the failure to follow safety policies that results in injury or death and the failure to plan for the achievement of every student entrusted to their care. By clearly defining the failure of responsibility, Stanford encourages principals to be guided by his military metaphor. "They must also feel a sense of responsibility for everything that happens under them," he says.

The military model is also at work in Stanford's habit of mind of framework, that provides his optimistic interpretation of the job's daily frustrations and disappointments. He describes his job as "being responsible for 50,000 children, one in which every day something will go wrong." So it is not unusual for Stanford to open the newspaper and see his picture beside an unflattering front-page headline.

He explains his framework for the challenge of his job with a crisp military metaphor. "What you see reported is, gee, Stanford is having a problem because he didn't get what he wanted at Sandpoint School. But keep in mind where I am. First there are tactics, second is strategy, and then there is something called the 'operative art.' " He details the difference: "Tactics are to win the little battles at individual schools; strategy is Seattle citizens, the school district, and what you do to win in this theater called Seattle. And the operative art is about how you win this whole war for democracy through public education."

The Tale of Two Metaphors

The metaphors Esther Torres and John Stanford use to create a point of view in their leadership recall John Gardner's provocative thesis in his book, *Leading Minds*. Gardner believes that leaders achieve their effectiveness chiefly through the stories they tell.[2] But leaders don't just tell stories, says Gardner; they also show them.

Viewed in this light, Torres and Stanford have woven the guiding metaphors of the farm and the military into their personal narratives as leaders. For Torres, the telling of "the farm story" becomes a way of establishing her uniqueness as a leader. Standing in a classroom of former foster youth, she holds up a diagram of a four-spoke wheel, and each spoke invokes a leadership lesson drawn from the farm. In this encounter with students, Torres both tells her story and embodies it.

When John Stanford tells and shows his story, his inner work involves a metaphor to create a connection between the experiences of a former army general and those of an educator. In telling his story, Stanford translates his military experience into a model to define leadership for himself and for the principals throughout the school system. Designer Tim Girvin tells his story—and creates a leadership model—from a very different metaphor.

Tim Girvin, CEO, Tim Girvin Design: Marketing a Zen Metaphor

Although you might not recognize Tim Girvin's face, you would recognize his handwriting. His company, Tim Girvin Design (TGD), has produced packaging and logos for Kraft's Macaroni, Chips Ahoy, American Express, Microsoft, and Planet Hollywood.[3] TGD has designed titles for more than 200 films, including *Apocalypse Now*, *Legends of the Fall*, and *Braveheart*.

Whether the product is a Mel Gibson film or packaging for Nabisco snack crackers, CEO Girvin's guiding metaphors as a leader can be traced to his twenty-five-year study of Zen Buddhism. Girvin's approach to both staff and clients reflects a Zen-inspired focus on meditation and searching for the "ch'i," or spirit, of an object. He uses these two metaphors to define his experience and enrich his resource of attunement.

Girvin was a student at Oregon's Reed College when he attended a lecture by Daisetz Suzuke, an American Zen priest and scholar from Japan. As Girvin remembers, "I became fascinated with the idea that the creation of art is a meditation—that the process of making something was as much a meditation as it was an expression."

This insight began Girvin's two-decade-long course of reading Zen philosophy and traveling through Asia. Further, the essence of this guiding metaphor persists in his approach to being in charge. "I think the whole puzzle of leadership is about meditation," he says, "because you can't arrive at a solution without contemplation. You need to come back to study, to meditate on the problem, and then arrive at what your next step might be."

Girvin has created a corporate culture that cherishes contemplation, from the shoji screens and scent of sandalwood in the conference room to the message he gives the leaders of the creative circles that form the nucleus of his organization. His advice for them connects contemplation and attunement. "Be quiet and listen," he says. "A lot of success has to do with listening, taking that information and thinking about it, and arriving at an outcome."

For Girvin, one Zen metaphor leads to another. The role of contemplation in his leadership involves him in getting to the essence of things. In Zen philosophy, this process is referred to as the search for the ch'i, or the spirit, of an object. And Girvin uses this metaphor to guide his company's creation of design and brand strategies for his clients.

The metaphor of ch'i inspired Girvin's trademark "Brandquest methodology." It is an exercise in attunement where a TGD employee learns about (contemplates) a new client's culture and products, meets with leaders, and talks to employees in order to capture the spirit of the company.

Girvin worked with client Clint Eastwood in a similar process to capture the ch'i of his film *The Unforgiven.* Eastwood gave Girvin the job description: Design a title logo to "capture the spirit of a man struggling in a brutal environment for redemption." Girvin contemplated the script and saw its cold, harsh spirit. The final, bold logotype was drawn with a steel pen on rough-hewn paper so that it appeared eroded, reflecting the spirit of the main character's struggle.

To talk to Girvin is to understand the guiding role of Zen metaphor in directing his experiences as a leader. As he explains, "My function is to get as close as I can to the center point of an organization, and find that central spirit—that spark, that central idea—and ignite it."

Has Girvin contemplated the ch'i of TGD? "I'm the spirit of the TGD brand," he answers. "As a leader of the organization, it is my function to act as the spirit or internal vision engine for the company."

The Model of Experience as Teacher

The experiences of Esther Torres, John Stanford, and Tim Girvin suggest two common threads. First, each of them has created a guiding metaphor by making a connection between dissimilar experiences. Torres connects a farmer's opening new channels in the field to creating community alliances and focusing the energy of foster youth. Stanford links shouldering responsibility as a soldier with taking the public's criticism as an educator and administrator. And Girvin sees similarities between his Zen contemplation of ch'i and his brainstorming for a brand strategy for his clients.

Next, note how these metaphors became models to direct each leader's experiences of being in charge. Finally, observe how leaders tell and show their symbolic stories, using them to establish their unique voices and strategies as leaders.

PC Connection CEO Pat Gallup offers one more metaphor, providing an image for understanding how much the world of experience teaches leaders. Gallup explains how her college major of primitive anthropology—the prehistoric environment—helped her understand the process of learning to lead. "Before written records, people had to learn by doing—by trial and error," she says.

Here's how Gallup leverages that lesson in her leadership. "Once you have good people and they have good basic training, you have to let them learn by doing. This means giving them the tools they need and letting them make the mistakes that come with learning from experience." Gallup's study of anthropology offers meaning in a metaphor that connects the experiences of the different leaders discussed in this chapter. "Some things," concludes Gallup, "you can't learn from a book."

The Exemplars: Models of Behavior

As the previous examples clearly show, powerful experiences outside the family are instrumental in shaping the legacy of a leader. This view of the world as a teacher recalls psychologist James Hillman's description of "the net of nurturance" that shapes our lives.[4] Far more than our parents influence our lives, insists Hillman, who offers a lyrical list of dimensions that nurture human development: the machines and interiors we live in, the food we eat, the music we hear, the streets and their sounds, the invisibles displayed by nature, and a vast array of people. "All this expresses the meaning of the world," says Hillman, "and each of us must respond."

Many leaders responded to their defining experiences by creating metaphors of meaning. Others encountered exemplars, or people along the path to leadership who served as models of leadership as a habit of mind.[5]

The leaders we have studied demonstrated that the much-used word mentor, with its focus on a short-lived sponsorship, does not reflect a teacher's lifelong influence on the legacy of a leader. In contrast, the word *exemplar* suggests how these very important people served as models of behavior, guiding the growth of inner resources in leaders-to-be.

These leaders underscore the observation made in Antoine de Saint-Exupéry's toddler text on leadership, *The Little Prince*.[6] As the fox tells the young royal, "All men have stars. For some, the stars are guides. For others, they are not more than lights in the sky." Consider three such stars as guides.

▪ Cathleen Black, now Hearst Magazines's president, began work for *Ms.* magazine publisher Patricia Carbine the day the first issue hit the stands in 1972. Carbine soon shared her view of Black's strengths, telling her, "Cathie, you can be practically whatever you want to be, so you ought to dream big dreams." Carbine's comment was both an invitation for Black to reflect on her strengths and an example of attunement. As Black explains, "From Pat Carbine, I learned that everyone is different, that each person can bring something to the party. But that you have to keep the bar high."

▪ Zion Prep principal Doug Wheeler was cooking hamburgers at Daly's Drive-In in Seattle when his third-grade teacher, Dr. Maxine Reynolds, stopped in. "What are you doing here?" asked Reynolds. Wheeler replied with pride, "I'm the manager." "That's not (expletive)!" she told him and walked out. Monday morning, when Wheeler came into work, his boss told him he no longer worked there and that he was to meet Dr. Reynolds on the campus of Seattle University, where she had enrolled him in the New Careers Project for low-income students. Today, in his role of school principal, Wheeler follows Reynolds's example, acting out of the conviction of urging children to reach their potential.

▪ Sallie Rowland, chairman and CEO of Rowland Designs and Indianapolis civic leader, fondly remembers Mrs. Heath, the junior high math teacher who detected Rowland had traced her mother's signature on her math homework. Confronting the artful forger, the teacher asked, "Wouldn't it be easier to just *do* the homework?" Years later, as a leader, Rowland still stresses this conviction about "doing the homework," urging her employees to create strong client presentations by being prepared.

Three leaders, three different exemplars. For Cathleen Black, Pat Carbine was a *discoverer*, or someone who recognized her potential as a leader and became a model for attunement and self-reflection. In Doug Wheeler's path to leadership, Dr. Maxine Reynolds was a *champion*, or a model of conviction. For Sallie Rowland, Mrs. Heath was an *instructor*, or a model for the habit of mind of conviction.

The Discoverers: Pointing to Potential

Earlier, we traced the family template of CIT Financial Group CEO Al Gamper. His father's loss of his job and lessons in tolerance inspired Gamper's convictions about avoiding class distinctions in leading CIT Financial Group. Just around the corner was another teacher, a retired banker who helped Gamper discover his potential and deepen his conviction about equal opportunity.

Gamper describes his discoverer, Arthur Boyd, as "a patrician, conservative, well-bred, private school, white-shoe guy. I was just the opposite. But he took a liking to me; he befriended me and offered me odd jobs, cutting his grass or painting his house. He would take me out to dinner, and we would talk about life, politics, and the business world."

When Gamper dropped out of Rutgers after his father became too ill to work, Boyd encouraged him to go into finance. Boyd introduced him to Phil Milner, a top executive at Manufacturer's Hanover Bank. This introduction started Gamper's financial career.

Once Gamper began his job at the bank, Boyd would take him out for drinks. With a double martini in hand, Boyd would remind Gamper of his potential and model his own convictions about equal opportunity. "I know you didn't go to Princeton or Yale," he once told Gamper, "but if you do a good job, a guy like you could run that place."

In recalling Arthur Boyd, Al Gamper describes both of the hallmarks of the discoverer exemplar. First, Boyd conveyed his belief in Gamper's potential, and then, like Al's dad, he offered a model of behavior that Gamper later expresses as "running CIT with an equity of how people are treated."

Another intriguing leader expands on Gamper's description of a discoverer, suggesting how a discoverer's actions can become a model for inner resources. Elaine Rosen, the president of UNUM America, the nation's leading disability insurer. Rosen was "discovered" by a star who became an essential guide and a model for the habit of mind of reflection.

Elaine Rosen, President, UNUM America: Lessons in Reflection

When Elaine Rosen succeeded Steve Center as president of UNUM America, they both knew the company would be in good hands, because Center had been her boss and discoverer almost two decades before. For Rosen, Center was an exemplar who modeled two behaviors that are key to reflection as a habit of mind: creating context and practicing self-observation. Both of these behaviors are critical to the ability to analyze and learn from one's experience.

Yet when Rosen first applied for a position as Center's management assistant, he turned her down. Center then dispatched someone from his department to offer her another job and tell her that they would be watching her. Six months later, when the new-hire quit, Center called her and asked, "Do you want the job now?"

"I said yes," remembers Rosen, "and so it began. There was something about me; I was able to see him as a wonderful teacher. Most people saw Steve as brash and impatient—a maverick rather than a mentor. But I was able to deal with him." She defines Center as a discoverer, because "he made me see what I had, told me what leadership qualities were, and made it clear what I had to learn."

One way Center conveyed his confidence in Rosen was to create a context for her to reflect about the bigger picture. She explains, "Being a management assistant involves a series of assignments. Steve would always show me the connection between the assignments, give me the issues, go over everything in his head. He would say, 'Do you follow me?' And if I said no, he would draw a diagram on the chalkboard or flip chart. He didn't just tell me about his ideas; he taught me how to think about this business. He always gave me context."

Rosen passes on this lesson in reflection: "I never ask anyone to do anything without context. I always give people a tremendous amount of information." She offers the example of the eighteen middle managers she would join for lunch later that day. Prior to this quarterly meeting, she sent them a package of what they call "Elaine's stuff"—a document from a competitor, a confidential memo from Wall Street. Once at lunch, she will invite them to analyze daily events in light of a larger picture.

Although Rosen traces this tutorial in reflection directly to Steve Center, she conveys the lesson with her own whip-smart sense of humor. When she spoke to 4,000 employees in her annual "State of the UNUM" speech, Rosen showed a clip from a *Seinfeld* episode, one in which the character Kramer can't live without take-out chicken from a neighborhood restaurant. She talked about customer loyalty and then segued to an audiotape of her conversation with an old customer and a new one.

At another meeting, she held up a photo of a local sandwich shop that had a handwritten ad in the window: "Full-time help, full benefits, HMO, 401K." Borrowing a quip from a Jack Nicholson movie, she told employees, "This is as good as it gets. If a sandwich shop is advertising job benefits, isn't this a terrific time for the kind of business we are in?" As Rosen puts it, "I always try to give them something bigger to think about."

Rosen also recalls how Steve Center modeled a second aspect of reflection, that is, teaching her how to observe and appraise her own behavior. As she admits, "I had a difficult time saying no, so I was always canceling meetings, overbooking, running late, or leaving early. I was never giving my full attention to where I was."

Center offered Rosen an unusual invitation: to see herself as others saw her. Rosen recounts this lesson in self-appraisal. "Steve said to me, 'It looks bad—coming late and leaving early. Leaders don't operate that way. When you go someplace, *be* there.' And from that day on, when I am in a meeting, I am present. I don't bring a cell phone or a beeper. I have learned to watch myself every minute of every day. Sometimes I feel like it is going to kill me. But I try to be like a duck, calm on the surface though paddling like mad under water."

In a similar way, Rosen now invites her employees to observe themselves. "If I have an employee who is not giving their people enough time, who is late, unprepared, or too political, I tell them what I observe. Then I explain why I think it makes them less effective. But, unlike Steve, I am not prescriptive; I try to get them to look at themselves and leave the change up to them," she says.

Summing up Center's lessons in leadership, Elaine Rosen offers a wonderful definition of a discoverer: "I knew that my career was as precious to him as it was to me."

The Blessing of Discovery

As the stories of Al Gamper and Elaine Rosen demonstrate, the blessing of a discoverer is twofold.[7] First, the discoverer believes in what he or she sees. Arthur Boyd and Steve Center each conveyed their beliefs in different ways: Boyd encouraged Gamper and shared his network, and Center offered Rosen an ongoing tutorial and tough feedback. As Rosen and Gamper saw themselves in the eyes of their discoverers, they saw their own potential as leaders.

Next, the discoverer serves as an exemplar, modeling behavior that each leader transforms and expresses in his or her unique point of view. Rosen teaches context with film clips, and Gamper strives for equity in his relationships at the CIT Financial Group.

The champion is a close cousin to the discoverer. These very important people are the exemplars who make and break the rules, open doors, sponsor, and steer leaders. Champions provide a model of behavior that leaders later transform into deeply held and strategic convictions.

How Champions Inspire Conviction

As with Zion Prep principal Doug Wheeler, whose third-grade teacher who got him fired from his job flipping burgers and enrolled him in college, many leaders have been inspired by the exemplars who have been their champions. For example, Rich Atlas sent Esther Torres to New York for an investment banking internship. Stephen J. Cannell, one of Hollywood's most prolific producers, also described a champion who served as a behavioral model.

Stephen J. Cannell, Chairman, Cannell Entertainment, Inc.: Turning the Lights On

Emmy-winner television writer and producer Stephen J. Cannell has created or cocreated more than forty television shows, including *The Rockford Files, Baretta, The A-Team, 21 Jump Street, Wiseguy,* and *The Commish*. In addition to scripting 350 of the 1,500 episodes he produced, he is the author of several best-selling books, including *The Plan* and *Final Victim*.[8]

Cannell describes the teacher who championed his ability and how he translated this model into his convictions as a producer: "I was learning disabled—dyslexic. I flunked three grades before I got out of high school. I got Ds and Fs and had to stay after school and be tutored every summer. Twice, I had to leave my class and step backward while they all went forward." Frustrated by the demands of spelling and sentence structure required by his teachers, Cannell honed his storytelling verbally and earned a family nickname of "the storyteller."

Then, as a college student at the University of Oregon, Cannell met his champion. Writing instructor Ralph Salisbury offered a counterpoint to the rules that had undermined Cannell's creativity. Cannell remembers, "Instead of three misspelled words being a flunk, Ralph said to me, 'It doesn't matter if you can't spell, as long as I can read it. I don't want you to just use the words you can spell; I want you to use every word you know. If you do it phonetically, I will figure it out.' Salisbury said, 'I'm not here to teach you to spell. I want to teach you how to get wonderful thoughts down on paper so they move other people.' "

Cannell saw Salisbury as a champion of writers. Salisbury's model of criticism is one he brings to work every day. Cannell says, "I see how Ralph is responsible for the way I deal with other writers. I remember when we would read our stuff in front of the class, and he would forbid the first round to be negative. If you started bashing someone's work, he would say, 'Whoa. What do you like about his story?' He set the tone for criticism that was positive."

To Cannell, this positive approach underlined his business-owner father's reminder to "catch someone doing something right." And he has translated the leadership lesson in his own language: "I always start with what I call the 'Atta Boys.' If someone comes in with a script that is really off the money, I search for things to praise. I tell the writer, 'There is a lot that is really cool about this script; I got a lot of Atta Boys in here, like the line on page twelve that really made me laugh, but, we still have some work to do. Let's call this a really good first draft.' Then, the writer comes out of my office feeling juiced."

Cannell tells a story that sums up the essence of how a champion conveys his belief in a leader-to-be. "I remember a short story I wrote called 'And Keep Them All Like Gentlemen,' " says Cannell. "Ralph called me in and said, 'Steve, this is breakthrough stuff. You have moved to another level and I want you to know you have a real gift. You should never stop being a writer.' "

For Cannell, it was Salisbury who offered the gift. "He turned the lights on. It was the first time anybody ever said that to me. I had the equipment, but I had to develop my talent. He turned it all on for me," concludes Cannell.

Comparing Champions

The role of a champion in the legacy of Esther Torres, Doug Wheeler, and Stephen Cannell was to be both a gatekeeper and a cheerleader. In these examples, the impact of champions as models of conviction is clear. By guiding, sponsoring, and encouraging leaders-in-waiting, champions offer an invitation to become a champion. Through the process of inner work, each leader can accept the invitation in his or her own terms.

A final type of exemplar is the instructor. To understand the impressive ways leaders leverage early models of leadership, consider the unique relationship between a then-young man from Pennsylvania named Bill Shore and a youthful senator from Colorado. Bill Shore is now the cofounder and executive director of Share Our Strength (SOS), a revolutionary antihunger organization that creates new wealth without a dime of government funding.

Bill Shore, Founder and Executive Director, Share Our Strength: Lessons from a Leader

Of his decade serving on the senatorial and presidential campaign staffs of Colorado senator Gary Hart, SOS executive director

Bill Shore has written, "There were many teachers to learn from and admire, but there was only one headmaster and that was Gary Hart. The lessons I learned from Hart will, I suspect, last a lifetime."[9]

Rather than recalling how Hart's presidential front-runner status ended with a front-page photo of Hart and model Donna Rice, Shore remembers Gary Hart as an exemplar, or an instructor. For Shore, Hart provided a model of the resources of conviction and attunement, which Shore adapted to create the nation's leading and most innovative antihunger organization.

Shore describes one of Hart's core convictions and then explains how this value is the driving force behind SOS: "If you told Hart you could only do this or that, you were asking for trouble. He didn't like having two options. Hart was always rejecting the conventional wisdom, looking for some third alternative."

Shore remembers Hart's unconventional marching orders when he sent Shore on his first scouting trip to New Hampshire. "Remember the presidential election is two years away," Hart cautioned. "Our audience is not New Hampshire voters or even New Hampshire's democrats. We are campaigning for fifty people, maybe twenty-five. If we get the right twenty-five people at the core of our team, they will get the next hundred and twenty-five, and they'll get the next thousand. Politics is a series of concentric circles and the most important circle is the first."

In creating these concentric circles, Hart also modeled the importance of attunement. As Shore explains, "He had an incredible sense that there was something to learn from everybody. Whenever Hart did a question-and-answer session, he would treat a question from a baker or steelworker with the same degree of seriousness as he would a question from a Wall Street banker—even when we were really pressed for time."

Shore has transformed Hart's conviction about challenging the conventional wisdom and attunement to each person's value in his innovative vision for SOS. This organization grew out of Shore's personal response to the horrors of the Ethiopian famine of 1984.

In his compelling book, *Revolution from the Heart*, Shore offers a smart summary of how he hoped to avoid the conventional wisdom:

"The last thing I wanted to do was to start yet another organization that spent a lot of money just to beg for more money through shrill direct-mail solicitations or guilt-inducing photos of starving babies. Leftover wealth is not a sturdy foundation for a new vision. New, untapped dollars and resources needed to be brought to the effort; new wealth needed to be created."

Shore says, "The idea of creating new options was very much a part of my training with Hart. I wondered, 'Why do there have to be just two boxes—profit and nonprofit?' " So instead of competing for wealth to fight hunger, Shore created wealth in several ways. First, he established an essential first "circle of supporters" like Apple founder Steve Wozniak and renowned Chez Panisse chef Alice Waters and launched a series of highly profitable events called "Taste of the Nation" in which prominent chefs volunteer for food and wine tastings that raise close to $4 million each year.

Next, Shore asked writers, such as Pulitzer Prize–winning Anne Tyler, to share their strength by contributing to an anthology called *Louder Than Words*. The circle of writers created another concentric circle, resulting in the "Writers' Harvest" in which 800 writers in 200 cities read their writings to benefit hunger in the United States.

Finally, Shore created a groundbreaking partnership with American Express. At the time Shore approached American Express, the company was struggling to get restaurants to accept its higher transaction fees. To create a more favorable profile, American Express became a major sponsor of Taste of the Nation and later joined with SOS in the "Charge against Hunger" program. In this program, American Express donates three cents to SOS every time customers use their cards in November and December each year.

SOS reflects Bill Shore's remarkable transformation of Gary Hart's curriculum of unconventional wisdom. Instead of competing for dollars, he mobilizes industries and individuals to share the strength of their talents to fight hunger. Since its founding, SOS has distributed more than $45 million to antihunger groups worldwide. Inspired by Hart, the "headmaster," Shore created his own revolutionary model of community and a point of view about what it means to be a leader.

A World of Teachers: The Role of Models

In the ultimate adventure tale *The Odyssey*, the poet Homer chronicled a custom in ancient, nonegalitarian Greece: pairing boys with older men in the hope that they would emulate the values of these guides.[10] When Odysseus left home for the siege of Troy, he asked his friend Mentor to act as guardian of his young son, Telemachus. During Odysseus's ten-year absence, Mentor served as a teacher and adviser to the young man. And from time to time, Athena, the goddess of wisdom, would disguise herself as Mentor and appear in his stead.

Thus, the word mentor has become shorthand for sponsoring and teaching the next generation of leaders. Yet in our conversations with leaders, we found the notion of a mentor as a role model was too narrow to embrace the world of teachers that influence leaders. Instead, we discovered two distinct types of models that shape strong leaders.

First, leaders use experience as a model, creating guiding metaphors to define their experience. Then, they draw upon their relationship with exemplars—the discoverers, champions, and instructors—who offered models of behavior. Both of these models nurture the habits of mind that clarify the vision and decisions of exceptional leaders.

By discussing role models in this new way, we can avoid using the word internalization, the textbook term so often associated with role models.[11] Clearly, the ability to internalize important people and experiences is a major source of development as a leader. Still, the word suggests imitation. And when we listen to Esther Torres's fresh images from the farm or to Bill Shore's testing the ideas from headmaster Gary Hart, we witness an act of creation.

NOTEBOOK: THE WORLD AS TEACHER

As the director of the Community Development Corporation, Esther Torres translates a farming metaphor—"keeping an eye on the end of the matter"—into a resilient framework for interpreting the challenges of her leadership.

- Identify an experience in your growing-up years that has influenced the way you interpret disappointments and setbacks in your organization.

- Imagine describing this experience to your staff or team. Specify how you could use a metaphor or image from the story to underline the importance of a positive framework in the others' approach to their work.

For UNUM president Elaine Rosen, Steve Center is a discoverer who offered a model of reflection for observing her behavior and creating a context for her work.

- Describe a teacher, coach, or boss who discovered you, recognized your potential, or offered you an opportunity to lead. How do you (or could you) recognize talented people in your organization in a similar way?

- Identify a person in your present or previous work setting who, like Steve Center, provided a model of self-appraisal or creating context. What key behaviors indicate this habit of mind of reflection at work?

Producer and writer Steve Cannell found a champion in his writing instructor, Ralph Salisbury, whose attunement allowed him to look beyond Cannell's disability and offer a unique model of criticism.

- Name someone who has championed your ability, bent the rules, and opened doors for you. Or a leader who, like Ralph Salisbury, provided an example of "catching someone doing something right." How have you applied these examples in your leadership?

SOS director Bill Shore recalls Senator Gary Hart as an instructor whose unconventional conviction inspired Shore's vision for the innovative approach of SOS.

- Recall someone in your career path whose convictions have influenced your vision as a leader. Specify how you have translated these examples in your day-to-day actions as a leader.

Chapter 3

The Moments of Meaning

Translating Events into Commitments

C hicago Cubs president Andy MacPhail tells a story about a certain pastrami sandwich, offering a classic example of a moment of meaning. MacPhail spins the story: "We were sitting on the tailgate of my Ford, having a picnic before a football game at Northwestern. I was eating a delicious deli sandwich and drinking an ice cold beer. It was a beautiful day, I was among friends, and I thought, 'It doesn't get much better than this.' But five minutes later, a shiny new Volvo wagon pulls up—out comes the card table, linen tablecloth, silverware, wine, cheeses, and hot dishes. All of a sudden, my sandwich doesn't taste as good."

MacPhail reflects on the meaning of this moment. "I had to ask myself: 'What is going on here? I was perfectly happy five minutes ago—why is this sandwich not as good as it was a bite ago? Nothing has happened to this sandwich; what has happened to me?'"

The way MacPhail answers these questions—and applies them in his leadership—is the key to this chapter. We explore a final aspect of the legacy of leaders: the illuminating moments and life-changing encounters that shift their perspectives about being in charge. As you glimpse vivid, painful, or mirthful moments of meaning in the lives of leaders like Andy MacPhail, you can again open Huxley's window to view what leaders *do* with what happens to them. Each moment of meaning becomes a catalyst for the growth of a leader's habits of mind.[1]

"It's the Same Sandwich": Taking Charge of Perception

Several habits of mind are mirrored in the lessons MacPhail learned from this moment of meaning. First, he describes a powerful hybrid of framework and reflection. In explaining the importance of framing events, he says, "The picnic taught me that your perception of events is very important. If you are not careful and you don't discipline yourself, you can let the perception that someone else has more than you really diminish what you have. You have to be really self-critical and self-aware about what is influencing you—changing your perception or paradigm."

For MacPhail, this moment of meaning serves both as a reminder to reflect and as a guiding metaphor for an optimistic framework in his leadership. He says, "The story comes back to encourage me to undergo that kind of self-analysis and remember that although my perception of a situation may have changed, it is often still the same sandwich."

He also tells the sandwich story to help the Chicago Cubs's front-office folks put any media coverage in perspective. He observes, "There is so much media reporting on our game. The media tend to make heroes and villains—idiots and geniuses—out of people whose work ethic and moral behavior haven't changed from year to year. Whether the team is winning or losing, people in the front office can get seduced by the media label—depressed or elated by their press clippings." MacPhail's message to them: "The media evaluates things in a snapshot of time. Remember, it's still the same team."

Making sense of his experience with the sandwich also allows MacPhail to understand and be attuned to his players. He says, "The experience gave me empathy for what our players can go through." He gives the example of a player with a $3 million contract who is unhappy to learn of a player with comparable ability making $5 million. MacPhail continues, "Your first reaction is, what the hell, he's making three million! Then I remember, what the hell, it was a beautiful day; I had a great deli sandwich; and I made myself miserable."

MacPhail explains how he passes on this lesson in leadership: "The incident has helped me understand what's going through other people's minds when they make a paradigm shift—to understand what they are trying to deal with. Through their agents, or in direct conversation with a player, I often tell them the story and let them know how this is similar to what may be going on in their lives."

Three Elements of Meaning

Andy MacPhail's description of this lesson suggests how creative leaders can be in analyzing and learning from their experiences. For instance, he has transformed a simple story about a sandwich into rich habits of mind in his leadership.

MacPhail's tale also reveals several elements that are present in all of the illuminating moments of the leaders we have studied. First, as theologian James Loder has observed, *knowing is an event*.[2] A moment of meaning can best be viewed as a short-term scenario that yields long-term effects in a leader's life. Next, it is clear that the center of an event of knowing is a *convincing insight*. And, finally, as analyst Herbert Fingarette has observed, this convincing insight can lead to a *new commitment*.[3]

Consider how these elements crystallized three leaders' convictions.

Barbara Davis Blum, President and CEO, Adams National Bank: Knowing as an Event

Barbara Davis Blum, president and CEO of Adams National Bank, describes an elevator ride as a powerful event of knowing. Blum was a twenty-year-old student at the University of Kansas when she joined her father for dinner at the American Bar Association meetings in Kansas City. Blum's father was a prominent Republican attorney and a former delegate to the Bull Moose Convention who had attended President William McKinley's funeral.

She describes the scene: "As we waited for the elevator, we were in the center of this vortex. People were shaking his hand and congratulating him—on an article, on a case, or a panel. I always knew he was important in my world, but it was the first time I was aware of how important he was outside of my little world. I loved it; I wanted to be where he was, to be like him."

Blum defines being like dear old dad in terms of his habit of mind of conviction. "I admired all of the things he brought to the table," she says. "I wanted to be the kind of person people respected that much, someone who was educated and civic-minded, who worked hard and always did his homework, who realized that if you don't understand politics you can't make a difference."

Blum has applied this event of knowing in her own terms and in a different political party: "When people tell me I remind them of my father, they are referring to my accomplishments." (Barbara Davis Blum was director of the Environmental Protection Agency in the Carter administration and deputy director for the Carter-Mondale presidential campaign before chairing Adams National Bank.) She continues, "But instead of one career, like my father, I have had several. I wanted to be where he was and I have managed to be."

Bruce Hallett, President, Time, Inc.: A Convincing Insight

Bruce Hallett, president of Time, Inc., can still quote Little League coach and sportswriter Blair Hollie's encouraging words from a column describing the first time ten-year-old Hallett played third base. He recalls, "There was nothing more fun and wonderful than opening up a bundle of papers I was delivering and seeing what Blair had written about the team. He was a big man with a bad leg; he was incredibly generous with his kids."

Hallett also remembers the meaning he made of another message Hollie wrote, one delivered to him on the pitcher's mound. On that summer afternoon, Hallett kept losing control of the ball and throwing walks. Suddenly, he noticed Coach Hollie (who would usually use a cane to walk to the mound to deliver his advice) giving a note to one of the kids on the bench. The entire playing field watched as the teammate approached the mound and as Hallett opened Hollie's note. It read "You are fired."

Reflecting on the shame of that game, Hallett describes his convincing insight in this event of knowing. Clearly, he has leveraged his Little League lesson into a habit of mind of conviction that guides his leadership. His insight is wry and wise. "I have fully forgiven Blair for sending a messenger," says Hallett, "but it was a corrective lesson. I realized that in communicating bad news, you need to be very personal and get in front of people and try to give them a feeling for what you are deciding to do—even if it is at a disadvantage to them."

Gary Locke, Governor, Washington State: A New Commitment

Governor Gary Locke of Washington State made headlines as the nation's first Chinese-American governor. The legacy of his victory reveals a vivid moment of meaning and a fascinating fact: Locke's maternal grandfather worked as a houseboy one mile from the governor's mansion. "It took our family one hundred years to move one mile up the road," Locke observed on the eve of his inauguration, and move into the governor's residence. Yet another moment of meaning—a visit to his paternal grandmother—inspired Locke's lifelong commitment and conviction about our government's responsibility to take care of its citizens.

Locke remembers, "I was ten years old, the eldest son of five children, when my father took me to visit his gravely ill mother in Hong Kong. We found her living in an 8-by-8-foot hut compound. There were dirt floors in the hallway and a sewage-filled stream nearby. She had three benches built into the wall; at night she would roll out her bedding to sleep on a bench. From her hut, I could see the homeless on the hills of Hong Kong Island, living in cardboard and scrap metal shacks."

Thirty-five years later, Locke can describe this moment of meaning with surprising detail. For him, the visit was a powerful event of knowing, one that produced a firsthand convincing insight into the horrors of impoverished housing. Locke's insight was later translated into the conviction that grounds his leadership in legislation for decent living conditions and expansive human services.

The Elements of Meaning

In this trio of meaningful moments, three key elements reveal an essential source of each leader's habit of mind of conviction: knowledge as an event, the gaining of a new insight, and the beginning of a new commitment. Perhaps an MGM moment of meaning in the movie *The Wizard of Oz* can help summarize each of these elements. Imagine Dorothy's tenacious pup, Toto, who pulled back the velvet curtain to reveal that the all-powerful Wizard of Oz was hiding behind the special effects of smoke and mirrors.[4] "Pay no attention to the man behind the curtain!" commanded the defrocked wizard. But for Dorothy, the leader of the pack, the meaning of this moment was clear.

Think about Dorothy's encounter with the wizard as an event of knowing. At the center of this event is a sad but convincing insight. She has understood that Oz is "a very good man but a very bad wizard." And, finally, by the time she clicks the heels of her ruby slippers, Dorothy is describing her new commitment: "There is no place like home."

These elements can be explored in a different kind of knowing event, one that allows an exceptional leader to reconcile two contradictory points of view and bring new meaning to an old conflict.

Ellen Bravo, Codirector, 9 to 5: The Eureka Effect—A New Meaning for an Old Conflict

In her role as codirector of 9 to 5, the National Association of Working Women, Ellen Bravo continues a career-long conviction about speaking out and organizing for equal justice. Yet Bravo recalls a time when she took unequal opportunity for granted, and she describes how watching the civil rights movement became an event of knowing that helped resolve her conflicting views about social change.

Bravo was born in 1944, in the shadow of the Holocaust. She explains the meaning she made: "I am Jewish, and I always knew about the Holocaust. But I thought, 'People must have known this was happening. How could you have known and not done something?' I had always had the feeling that if there is something wrong, you must speak out."

Still, when fourteen-year-old Bravo's father was in an accident and her mother could barely support the family, she felt conflicted about this inequity. "I wondered why my mother's income was so little, even though she did important work," remembers Bravo. "I believed in speaking out, but there were also things I took for granted: that women made less money and their work was of less value than men, and that some people had lots of money and some had very little. I thought what happened in my family was just the way the world worked."

Bravo's first response to the conflict was to enroll in college and become a scholar of Greek and Latin. As she puts it, "I wanted to leave behind the grubby world of regular life. But I quickly discovered that the world of scholarship was just as grubby." Bravo's stint as a classics scholar coincided with the beginning of the civil rights movement. And as she watched, she understood how to resolve her conflict about speaking out.

Bravo describes her moment of meaning: "What changed was when I saw the civil rights movement on the news. I saw people being hosed. Then I saw people being beaten and then getting up and becoming part of a bigger crowd. Then I saw laws being changed. I began to feel that things could be different. I always felt that if I saw an injustice I would speak out against it; but I didn't understand how much the things I saw were injustices that could be changed. So rather than withdrawing from the world, I saw how I could now get very much involved in changing it."

Arthur Koestler, who chronicled creativity, might have called Bravo's meaning making an act of "bio-sociation." When her two incompatible points of view merged, they composed a new and unified view of the world.⁵ Theologian James Loder might choose a more light-handed label, because Bravo is an example of what he calls "the Eureka Effect."⁶ When her conflicting ideas were resolved, Bravo experienced a release of energy that had been bound up in the conflict. This energy was then available for testing the original conflict in light of her new resolution.

Bravo's resolution of her conflict contains all three elements of a moment of meaning. Watching the civil rights movement on the news was an event of knowing that yielded a convincing insight: Injustice can be changed. This insight led to Bravo's commitment to social change, a conviction that is at the heart of her leadership of 9 to 5.

The Meaning of Family

Ellen Bravo, Governor Gary Locke, and Barbara Davis Blum illustrate how the imprint of family can be reflected in moments of meaning. In earlier chapters, we have described many events of knowing in the circle of a young leader's family. Recall just two: At eight years old, PC Connection CEO Patricia Gallup saw her father returning home at dawn with blistered hands and lungs after fighting a neighbor's house fire; and eleven-year-old Doug Wheeler, now the principal at Zion Prep Academy, after declaring that only the "real children" could get cereal, heard his father's sermon about what it means to be a family.

Each leader connected with a convincing insight and a new commitment in their moment of meaning. In watching her father, Gallup understood the importance of "treating people right," and today she links the meaning she made to her passionate habit of mind of being attuned to and exceeding customer expectations. Wheeler also drew upon his essential insight to create a new commitment, saying, "When I came downstairs, I understood the power of being all one family, and I knew I would never exclude family members again." As a leader, this moment of meaning is central to his conviction that his school must be willing to "be a family for each child."

The meaning of family is also conveyed by Beckie Masaki, executive director of the Asian Women's Shelter in San Francisco. She describes a stunning event of knowing that took place as she looked at her mother's high school yearbook and as she understood the meaning of her parents' internment in World War II.

Beckie Masaki, Executive Director, Asian Women's Shelter: Bicultural Conviction

As a young child, Beckie Masaki received many clues about her parents' imprisonment in a Japanese internment camp in World War II. She says, "My parents would gloss over their internment, but I could fill in the blanks. One of them would say, 'Your grandfather used to own this business, but he had to sell it during the war.' Or 'We had to move out of that house; we lost it because of the war.' "

But Masaki's moment of meaning came as she looked at her mother's high school yearbook. She remembers, "Looking at her yearbook, it came as a shock to learn that she had graduated from high school in the internment camp. I had seen my older cousin's yearbook—the students on the green lawns—and I had watched high school kids on television shows. But the pictures in my mother's yearbook showed students standing in front of desolate barracks in the desert. This was my first picture of my parents' experiences during the war."

For Masaki, this illuminating moment allowed her to imagine and to gain a convincing insight about her parents' life in the camps. "I saw what my mother's life was like; I imagined her as a teenager living there," she says. Masaki's event of knowing was also the beginning of a new commitment to social justice and to seeing the world through what she calls "bicultural lenses." Wearing these lenses became a habit of mind and a source of her conviction and inner authority.

As she explains, "Looking back, I see the roots of my commitment to social justice came from knowing that my family was put into those camps. It was dissonant to me; it didn't fit in with what I knew about my parents as good citizens and good people."

Her mother's yearbook suggested stories that weren't told in Masaki's history books. "The fact that my parents were in prison made a big impression on me," says Masaki. "It was the beginning of my thinking critically about injustice in our society. So much of our schooling is based on mainstream culture. It doesn't relate to my experiences as a person of color. Thinking about internment is where I learned to do critical thinking about injustice. It was the roots of my seeing that I needed to have bicultural lenses—to learn not to swallow things whole."

The view through her bicultural lenses allowed Masaki to trust her inner authority about and address the need for a shelter to serve Asian victims of domestic violence. In the late 1980s, Masaki was working at Casa de las Madres in San Francisco, one of the first women's shelters in the nation. When Masaki asked the director why no Asian women came to the shelter, she was told that domestic violence was not a problem in the Asian community. "I had no statistics to prove they were wrong, but the general mythology was a disconnect for me. It didn't match my own experience in the community," says Masaki. Her insight began the process of creating the country's first shelter for Asian women.

Masaki's critical thinking, born in her moment of meaning, enriches her capacity to rely on her inner authority as a habit of mind in her leadership. As she sums up her strategy: "We don't allow the status quo or conventional pressure to create our organization. When someone calls us to give up consensus management and create a hierarchy, I encourage the group to ask: Does this fit our philosophy of how we want to work? We must question the truth of conventional perspectives to create a truly good fit for our organization."

The Metaphors of Meaning

Like Andy MacPhail, many leaders translate a knowing event (the Volvo with the superior picnic) into a guiding metaphor ("It's still the same sandwich") of their leadership. Consider the example of Harvey Jones, chairman and CEO of Cutter and Buck, Inc., a premier golf apparel company recently named by *Business Week* as one of the "100 companies to watch."

Jones describes a moment of meaning that evolved into a guiding metaphor. It is an image that shapes his optimistic framework when he faces a daunting challenge as a leader. He remembers, with remarkable clarity, the sunny August day when he was nine years old and stood at the end of the high diving board.

Having spent the summer envying the courage of the older kids, leaping and doing cannonballs into the water, Jones decided to take the plunge. But when he stepped to the edge of the board, he froze with fear and decided to go back down the ladder. When he turned and saw the long line behind him, he knew he couldn't turn back. So he walked the plank and jumped. As he emerged from the water, it hit him: He had done it! It was the scariest thing he had ever done, but he had survived.

This guiding metaphor continues to guide Jones's leadership and strengthen the habit of mind of framework, or his ability to interpret negative events. Jones explains, "Whenever I face a change or challenge that requires a risk, I picture myself standing at the end of the high diving board. And I tell myself, 'It's just jumping off the high dive.' Then, I can welcome the challenge and jump."

Meaning by Example

Earlier, we detailed a number of exemplars whose behavior created an event of knowing. For example, conductor Leonard Bernstein singled out new trumpeter Gerard Schwarz for praise, which prompted Schwarz to reflect and create a new commitment not to single out players at the expense of the orchestra.

The role of exemplars in moments of meaning is well described by Bill Mays, president of Mays Chemical Company, in his recollection of a 1973 meeting with the Midwestern industrialist, former Republican National Committee chairman, and Cummins's Engines chairman of the board, J. Irwin Miller. At the time of this event of knowing, Mays was a new college graduate and in his first job as assistant to the president at Cummins Engines in Columbus, Ohio. Also present at the meeting was the executive vice president, James Joseph, who later served as U.S. ambassador to South Africa.

The agenda of the meeting included deciding whether Cummins Engines should divest its resources in South Africa. As Mays listened to the board's discussion and its subsequent decision to sell Cummins's facilities in South Africa, despite the financial losses involved, Mays gained a convincing and clear insight. "My conclusion was that when leaders make the hard decisions, they are responsible for doing what is right—not just what is profitable."

Like his exemplar Irwin Miller, who once waited a month in Brazil for a company phone to avoid paying a kickback, Mays now bases his corporate policies on principle and not just on profit. Describing the general benefits package he offers employees at Mays Chemical, he says, "They might cost me more, but they give peace of mind to my employees. I have to do what is in the best interests of my people—not just from a pure business perspective."

What ties the stories of Mays and Schwarz together is that each exemplar initiated a moment of meaning in the model of their behavior. In Schwarz's knowing event with Bernstein, the meaning issued a caution. For Mays, Miller's example served as an inspiration. In both examples—and this is the crucial point for our discussion—the insight from the knowing event led to a new and long-standing commitment.

In a final story, the insight from an event of knowing motivated Scott Oki, Microsoft's international vice president, to leave the company when he was widely considered to be its next president.

Scott Oki, President, Oki Foundation: More to Life Than Microsoft

"I mean, how do you say no to Bill's mother?" wondered Microsoft executive vice president Scott Oki in 1991, when Mary Gates invited him to join the Foundation Board of the Children's Hospital in Seattle. Oki agreed, and his participation became a knowing event that led to a dramatic change in his commitment to work, family, and community.

Oki describes his central insight: "Joining the Children's board was a key trigger point—a watershed event—planting the idea that there is more to life than working eighty hours a week at Microsoft. Microsoft demanded a maniacal work focus: If you were awake, you were expected to be thinking about Microsoft. But once I figured out there are other interesting things to do outside of Microsoft, it triggered a thought process that led me to conclude there were other things I should be spending my time on. It started me thinking about what I wanted to do in the community."

For ten years, Scott Oki had been "spending his time" at Microsoft. He joined the company in 1982, when it had 120 employees.[7] Oki soon created a business plan to launch an international division and worked three years without a day off, logging 400,000 frequent flyer miles in a single year. His results were a stunning success. Within four years, Microsoft's international division accounted for 42 percent of revenue and 50 percent of the company's profits.

From his seat on the Children's Hospital Foundation Board, Scott Oki began to see what he calls his "dog years" at Microsoft in the context of his life both at work and at home. Clearly, his participation stimulated his habit of mind of reflection, and he engaged in a vigorous self-appraisal. As he examined and resolved his contradictions about work, community, and family, he experienced the Eureka effect.

Oki's reflections are careful and candid. "At the time I served on the board, my wife, Laurie, and I had one child and one on the way. This put my participation into sharper focus. I had to ask, What are my priorities? How much of my identity is tied up here? I knew that my management style was one of management by example. If I wanted people to work eighty hours a week, I had better be doing the same. Yet, being a good husband and father is pretty incompatible with those hours. I knew I would feel conflicted and guilty if I was at home and not in the office, and guilty if I was in the office and not at home."

How did Oki, who many speculated would be the next president of Microsoft, decide to call it quits? He resolved his contradictions. "Life is too short to be living on a big guilt trip," he explains. "I concluded that money was not an issue and that Microsoft was not so much a part of me that I would lose my identity or reason to live when I left. I had realized that there were a lot more things to do in my life."

One year after his event of knowing on the Children's Hospital board, and four months after his second son, Nicholas, was born, forty-three-year-old Oki left the mouse race with a reported 500,000 shares of Microsoft stock. "The hardest part was telling Bill," says Oki.

No matter how you do the math, you can see that Oki had considerable capital to refocus his energy and spend time with his family and community. His first new opportunity began after the birth of his second son, when his wife complained about the lack of reasonably priced baby blankets. After market-oriented Oki studied the field and reported a great business opportunity, Laurie teased him, "I thought you were planning to retire."

But Oki continued to think about the profit potential of baby blankets. Then he read an article about actor Paul Newman's foundation. For Oki it was another moment of meaning that helped resolve his contradiction about retirement and involvement. "Newman was giving away 100 percent of the profits from his pasta sauce, popcorn, and pretzels to various charities. It made me think, 'Wouldn't it be great if we could do that with baby blankets? We could combine high quality and profit, and give 100 percent to children's charities,' " he remembers.

Thus, Nanny and Webster, a company that manufactures affordable baby blankets, became a premier for-profit project of the Oki Foundation, which supports child-related causes in the Seattle area. Oki, who also serves on twenty nonprofit boards, describes the foundation's mission: "to marry my passion for things entrepreneurial with my passion for things philanthropic in a way that encourages others to do the same." As the product of that marriage, Nanny and Webster employs handicapped and disabled people to package its product, and Oki contributes 100 percent of the gross profits to children's charities.

Scott Oki's story reveals the influence of a powerful event of knowing. Mary Gates's invitation to become a member of the Children's Hospital board was the beginning of a habit of reflecting about rebalancing business, family, and community. It is a process that came full circle when Oki served as president of the Children's Hospital Foundation Board.

Pentimento: The Meaning of Legacy

The powerful meaning of a leader's legacy of family, teachers, and knowing events can be summarized by borrowing a guiding metaphor from writer Lillian Hellman's autobiography, *Pentimento.*[8]

Hellman wrote, "Old paint on canvas, as it ages, sometimes becomes transparent. When that happens, it is possible, in some pictures, to see the original lines: a tree will show through a woman's dress, a child makes way for a dog, a large boat is no longer on the open sea. That is called pentimento because the painter 'repented,' changed his mind. Perhaps it would be as well to say that *the old conception, replaced by a later choice, is a way of seeing and then seeing again.* That is what I mean about the people in this book. The paint has aged now and I wanted to see what was there for me once, what is there for me now."

Similarly, we have asked each leader in this book to look at their legacy and, then, to see it again. As mature leaders whose paint has aged, they show us the original lines—the people and events that were there for them once—and the habits of mind that are here for them now. They have transformed old conceptions into later choices. They draw upon their legacies to create the art of their leadership.

NOTEBOOK: THE MOMENTS OF MEANING

Chicago Cubs president Andy MacPhail's statement, "It's still the same sandwich," describes his lesson at a tailgate picnic about choosing a positive perception of events.

- Recall a similar event, one where your perception of the event was directly related to your ability to tackle the situation. Summarize your insight about this experience in one memorable phrase.

- Detail a recent challenge or change in your organization. Compare your framework in meeting this challenge with MacPhail's resilient approach.

Governor Gary Locke's youthful glimpse of his grandmother's impoverished housing in Hong Kong was an illuminating moment that he later translated into his conviction about affordable housing and human services.

- Identify an experience that shifted your perspective and was a catalyst for the growth of your convictions as a leader.

For Scott Oki, his participation on the Children's Hospital board was a defining moment that led to his leaving Microsoft and creating a new commitment to the replenishment of family and community.

- Specify a person or an experience that shifted your perspective about work and family life. How did you incorporate this new direction in leading your organization?

Consider James Loder's observation that knowing is an event, one with a central and convincing insight.

- Describe an illuminating event in your private or professional life. What is the central insight from this experience that you have applied to your leadership?

- How did (or could) this insight lead to a new commitment or enrich a habit of mind in your leadership?

Part Two

Habits of Mind

The Resources to Inform and Invigorate Leadership

Chapter 4

Reflection

Examining Experience

P rinceton University professor and president Dr. Harold Shapiro gives his family high marks for providing an unhurried childhood, one that allowed him time to nurture the habit of reflection. As Shapiro explained, "I really thank my parents for not getting me as busy as kids are today, running from music lessons to French lessons to soccer practice. My parents had no notion of those things. So I had a lot of time to myself, and it gave me time to speculate and reflect. My best times as a child were spent sitting on a curb watching a caterpillar in the grass, and wondering where it came from or where it was going, and then looking up 'caterpillar' in the encyclopedia."

For Shapiro, the lesson from the caterpillar is clear. "As I sat on the curb, thinking about things around me, I learned that some of life's greatest treasures are at hand if you examine your experience instead of just allowing it to happen to you. I learned from early childhood on that you could really examine your current experiences and gain strength from that examination."

Harold Shapiro and his twin brother, Bernard, grew up in Montreal in a warm extended family in which examining experiences was a family ritual. Their father, Max, was a tinsmith by trade who emigrated from Poland to America in 1912. He hoped to send for his wife and two children, but he later learned that only his daughter had survived World War I.[1] Settling in Montreal, Max became part owner of Ruby Foos, one of the city's most popular restaurants.

Through his second marriage to Mary Tafler, Max joined a family that argued and examined their experiences. Harold Shapiro remembers the family's Friday night Sabbath dinners with full-throated arguments about why Harold and Bernard were going to private school, whether movies should be censored, and why their participation in the community was important.

As a child, Shapiro wondered if his ruminating relatives "disliked each other." Yet years later, during a postcollege short stint running Ruby Foos with his brother, he made this legacy his own. Every Monday night, Harold's friends met at the restaurant for a free meal and began heated discussions—for instance, whether Bach or Beethoven had more to offer—that often moved from Ruby Foos to Shapiro's apartment.

Harold Shapiro has translated a legacy of reflection to strengthen his resolve as a leader. As we explore reflection as a powerful habit of mind, we detail how leaders examine their behavior and learn from their experiences.

Reflections: The New President in Town

Within months of moving to Princeton University from the University of Michigan, President Harold Shapiro swiftly sharpened the budget ax. In response to a projected deficit of $1.8 million in Princeton's budget, he proposed to trim $6 million over the next five years. To some, this deficit was merely a drop in Princeton's $394 million budget's bucket, but as Shapiro surveyed his new setting, he saw the potential for the deficit to multiply, especially with the community's great expectations about Princeton's purchasing power. As he explains, "I realized there were expectations out there that exceeded the wildest estimates of our financial capacity."

Even though the cuts were small, mostly administrative costs, the uproar was huge. In the hand-wringing and finger-pointing that followed, faculty members demanded to know why Princeton— which had just completed a $410 million endowment campaign— was so strapped. Couldn't the deficit be covered by taking more from the endowment? Others complained about the mixed messages. "We started out from the feeling that we were a rich university that could do everything, and then suddenly we were told we were poor and couldn't do anything," said one faculty member.

Another faculty member described Shapiro's actions as "a failure of salesmanship and communication." Dr. Shapiro responded by apologizing to the faculty for the "unnecessary confusion and anguish" caused by the budget review and by taking responsibility for the failure to convey his reasoning behind it. When he reflected on this fracas, Shapiro revealed both his capacity for self-observation and how he has applied the lessons from this experience.

"Like anyone coming to a new situation, I saw things that others didn't see," Shapiro says, "My own view was that the people at this university—like so many others—had told themselves for so long how wonderful and well off they were that they really believed it. But it was clear to me that over the long term we were in an untenable situation, and adjustments had to be made. Still, if I had to do it over again, I would have waited a while—because we weren't actually in a crisis—and until I had built up more trust here. I think it was an error to have moved so quickly."

These days, Shapiro can scarcely walk across the campus without someone praising him for getting the budget under control. Yet his observations about himself and the situation are fair and unflinching: "It doesn't matter how good you are, people had experienced a loss, because they had an enormous investment in the previous administration. They had a set of connections, understandings, and a way of dealing with the administration. I wasn't sufficiently sensitive to people's loss when I came here. I think a little waiting would have helped a lot."

Shapiro applies the lesson of this experience in a habit of mind that directs his leadership. "I remind myself that in all learning, trust is important. Faculty, staff, and administration are always learning from each other," states Shapiro. "Therefore, you must ask yourself again and again, 'What is the level of trust? Is it enough to make sensible judgments and have people live with them?' "

Consider, too, how Shapiro's habit of reflection creates context in understanding his experiences of being in charge.

Putting Prejudice in Context

Growing up in Montreal, where Jewish children were not welcome in the public schools, Harold and Bernard attended Lower Canada College, a nearby private school. As Shapiro recalls, "I knew from an early age that there were people who had these kind of prejudices, and I would have to make my way in spite of the barriers."

Shapiro's reflections about barriers allowed him many years later, as a university president, to put issues of prejudice into a larger context. He says, "My reflection was that I had to unlearn my own lessons, to understand how my experience was not really a good guide. It did teach me to be sensitive and generous to others who were being discriminated against. But the kind of prejudice to which Jews have been subjected in North America was qualitatively different than the prejudices that African Americans, Hispanics, and Asian Americans face at this stage of history."

Upon reflection, Shapiro knew he had to learn something new. "Because the experience of African Americans was so different, I had to learn to understand this all over again," explains Shapiro. Was there a moment of meaning that helped Shapiro understand? "No single event, but when I was at the University of Michigan, I talked with colleagues, listened to debates, and tried to immerse myself in the history of other experiences as best as a stranger could," says Shapiro.

We can witness the ripening of Shapiro's reflections about prejudice by returning to a portrait of a student protest at the University of Michigan, reported earlier in the Introduction. To reset the scene: Following a screaming match between the board of regents and a large group of students about divestiture of the university's portfolio in South Africa, Shapiro wondered, "Is there something here worth understanding?" He then invited the students into his office.

Listening to the students changed his mind. Shapiro explains how his decision came from understanding a larger context: "The meaning I made is that race has a very special set of messages in America. African Americans have been discriminated against for so long in this country that they had developed a set of strategies and structures that enabled them to survive this awful discrimination. And even though I thought those strategies would no longer serve them well in the world that was unfolding, I thought we had to pay attention to them and acknowledge them—even if it meant doing things that, in some abstract way, didn't make sense to us."

As he reflected about what the students told him, Shapiro still didn't think that moving U.S. firms out of South Africa was helpful in the long run to the people in South Africa. "But it was helpful to people in America," he believes. His bottom line: "I don't think it helped South Africa, now or then. But what it did was help black-white relations in this country, and that was worth investing in. Because of our history and the necessity of providing more empathy for each other, I thought it was well worth it."

For Harold Shapiro, reflection is part of a family legacy that offered him time to reflect and whose Sabbath dinner discussions modeled the art of examining experience. It is also a legacy and habit of mind he wishes to pass on to a new generation of students. His first-year students in a class called "The Aims of Education" echo Shapiro's early curbside musings, the Sabbath dinner discussions, and the late-night debates at Ruby Foos.

"He doesn't ask just questions of fact," says student Shoshanan Lopatin.[2] "He asks us, 'How do you feel about that? Or what are the implications?' Discussions don't stop even when the class ends. We walk across the campus still deep in discussion."

The Rudiments of Reflection

Dr. Harold Shapiro's stories suggest how leaders use reflection as a habit of mind to engage experience in several distinct ways. Shapiro's self-observation was at work in his hindsight about the budget-cutting debacle at Princeton. Through his appraisal of his actions, he was able to apply the lesson of the experience and use trust as a tool for testing the climate for change. In his decision about divestiture at the University of Michigan, his reflections allowed him to cast his understanding of prejudice in a larger context.

The rudiments of Shapiro's recollections demonstrate how the resource of reflection organizes a leader's experiences. But how is reflection different from introspection? And how is a moment of meaning different from reflection as a habit of mind?

The second question can be quickly dispatched. The difference resides in the word *habit.* Moments of meaning are short-lived, illuminating events or eras leading to the insights that create long-term commitments in leaders' lives. Reflection is a resource leaders use to examine day-to-day experiences. Reflection is a habit of mind, as opposed to a mind-changing event.

Introspection or reflection? Neither can be dismissed as bell-bottom naval gazing. Both require self-examination, and both demand an internal dialogue.[3] Yet introspection is a kind of pure research in which observing and exploring the nature of your experience becomes an end in itself. Think of poet Elizabeth Barrett Browning examining her experience with Robert Browning and asking, "How do I love thee? Let me count the ways. . . ."

By contrast, reflection is applied research using participant observation. Leaders who seek knowledge of their own actions and reactions create a means to understanding their impact on others. Think of Harold Shapiro in the heat of a student protest asking himself, "Is there something here I should be understanding?"

Two leaders illuminate these distinctions: Neil Braun, the president of NBC Television, and David Giuliani, CEO of Optiva Corporation, whose Sonicare toothbrushes have made it one of the fastest-growing companies in the United States. In both cases, the ability of each leader to observe his own behavior was essential to the applied research of reflection.

Neil Braun, President, NBC Television: The "Just in Case" Book

For NBC Television president Neil Braun, the sudden death of Showtime's forty-three-year-old president Tony Cox was the catalyst for fulfilling a promise he had made when his daughter was born: to keep a journal of his reflections. "I wanted to make sure I had communicated to her all the things that are important to me, the different ways I have learned to think, and the life lessons I have learned," says Braun. "I call it my 'Just in Case' book, and I carry it with me all the time."

Among the journal's entries are his reflections about a lesson taught by his exemplar, Frank Biondi, and an entry about what he learned from being teacher for a day at Peter Stuyvesant High School in New York. Both reflections display Braun's capacity to observe himself and then apply the lessons of his experiences.

Braun recalled his first performance review with Frank Biondi, then president of Viacom. When Braun asked him for a review, Biondi said, "Why do you need one? You are doing a great job." But Braun insisted, asking, "What do you wish I had done better, quicker, differently?" Biondi's two-part response provided Braun with what he called "the definition of a perfect boss," one he applied within minutes of the meeting's end.

Here's what Biondi told Braun: "I decided long ago to evaluate people on two simple things. The first is trust, meaning integrity and judgment. I know you have integrity because I checked your references and judgment you earned over the years. The second is effectiveness. And whatever I ask you to take on, you always get done. So, if I trust you, and you get things done, nothing else matters."

Returning to his office, Braun reflected on his moment of meaning with Biondi. Braun remembers, "It was a real epiphany for me, because I realized that I didn't manage that way." He immediately called in one of his managers and told him about this lesson, saying, "I realize that I have been managing you by trying to remake you into me. But you are different from me, and good at things I'm not good at. So from now on, let's be partners and keep each other in the loop."

Braun explains how this event of knowing developed into a reflective habit of mind that reminds him to appreciate diverse viewpoints: "When I hire someone, I tell them, 'I have checked out your integrity, and I want to be able to trust you. I will see your judgment as you solve problems. But if you do it differently than I would, it's an advantage to the organization.' "

For Braun, the encounter with Biondi helped him apply a lesson about a kind of diversity that is not defined by color and gender. "It is about diversity of thought and experience," says Braun. "I love to learn new ways to think from people around me." And the diverse ideas of students at Peter Stuyvesant High School offered Braun another opportunity to apply the research of reflection.

When television journalist Jane Pauley asked Braun to volunteer to be a teacher for a day at Stuyvesant, he elected to teach a values and ethics class. Using the Socratic method he remembered from law school, he challenged students about whether it was possible to find a balance between success and happiness. The class was a hit, with students staying long after the bell, and Braun rode back to NBC wondering if he should quit his job.

As he recalls, "I was thinking, 'I have to become a teacher!' It was the most empowering day I ever had. I was so impressed with the level of insight, mutual respect, and intellectual honesty; there was so much tolerance for all of their different ideas." When he returned to the office, Braun continued to reflect: "I don't want to leave my job—because I love it—but what I really want to do is to bring the feeling I had in the classroom back to my job."

Upon reflection, Braun understood that the key to applying his experience was honesty. "The hardest things about having this title is getting people to tell you the truth," explains Braun, who put his high school lesson to work in several concrete ways. First, he told his Stuyvesant story at the next "town meeting" with the whole division.

Braun told the employees, "I'm going to do everything I can to convince you that behind closed doors is an appropriate time for you to tell me what you think. I'm too insulated from what goes on here, and I really value those of you who come in and tell me what you think can be done better." He promised, "I will never penalize you for telling me what you think."

Then he changed the conversation at a monthly breakfast meeting with several dozen folks from the network division. Instead of fielding the group's politically careful questions, he invited them to tell the truth, saying, "Come on, I know what you really want to ask me about is job security. So let's talk about job security."

Braun transformed his reflections into his actions as a leader. As he puts it, "I try to cut to the unspoken, the stuff I know they are afraid to put on the table. I find that shining the light on it and putting it in perspective helps them understand a bigger context and helps prepare them for what is coming next."

David Giuliani, CEO, Optiva Corporation: Applying the Lessons of Experience

In the early 1990s, Optiva CEO David Giuliani was an executive at Abbott Chemical and was spending most of his free time in his garage, tinkering with a prototype for a sonic toothbrush.[4] Discouraged by the power the brush required and the breakage of the ceramic strip holding the clump of its bristles, Giuliani was ready to quit.

Then Giuliani took a walk on the beach, watching the waves wash over the sand and eroding the beach. He began to reflect: If it works on the beach, why wouldn't it work in the mouth? Why couldn't sound waves travel through fluid to erode plaque away? Thus began the creation of a new prototype—a toothbrush–tuning fork driven by a vibrating electromagnetic field—and a new product and company that would be feted by the White House, endorsed on *Oprah*, and chart a five-year growth rate of 31,507 percent.

For David Giuliani, the same habit of mind of reflection that allowed him to link the seascape to a Sonicare toothbrush was also a rich resource in his leadership. Two examples from Giuliani's early childhood and career illuminate his inner work in applying the lessons from his experiences.

Giuliani's family template includes a mother who modeled reflection. As he recalls, "My mother was a pretty amazing woman. At twenty-four years old, during World War II, she signed up as a social worker for the American Red Cross and worked in New Hebrides and Australia. She was a constant source of observations; she would always comment on things. So I got to see how she thought, see how her mind operated. She showed me lots of reactions that colored the world." And it was his mother's comments about his sloppy homework that taught Giuliani a lesson he applies in his leadership.

Giuliani remembers a time at age 10 when he finished his homework well past bedtime only to have his mother inform him that he "really ought to make this neater." Giuliani admits, "My first reaction was, 'I'm happy with it, get lost,' or some polite version of that." Then his mother explained the importance of her standards and showed her willingness to help him tidy up his report. His second reaction was one of reflection: "I realized, hey, if she is willing to put her time and energy into making this neater, and invest in it, maybe I should, too. So I stayed up an extra hour."

How is this ancient lesson about homework reflected in Giuliani's leadership at Optiva? Giuliani linked his mother's lesson to a strikingly similar situation with a newly hired, highly capable young executive who produced a poorly developed proposal. As Giuliani recalls, "I could have accepted it, because the issues she needed to justify were obvious, but it seemed to me that this was a teaching opportunity. So I sent the proposal back to her four or five times with comments, and each time she worked on it."

After the fifth draft, Giuliani sent the proposal to the board without comment. When a board member sent an e-mail praising her work, she demanded to know if Giuliani had prompted his praise of her proposal. "I didn't say a word," Giuliani told her. "He has no idea how much agony you went through to bring it to this level."

Commenting on the link between his past and present experience, Giuliani says, "There are two important points here. One is telling the truth, and the other is being able to take the time to be involved and to teach—not just for the business at hand—but for growth, for on-the-job training."

In reflecting on his first job—a twelve-year stint as an engineer at Hewlett-Packard (HP)—Giuliani says, "I grew up at Hewlett-

Packard. The voices of my mentors at HP still live on as little voices in my head." We see how he has applied the lessons of his experience of HP's famed "worker friendly" culture. For instance: Optiva provides its workers—60 percent are immigrants from Southeast Asia, Eastern Europe, Latin America, and Africa—with an English-as-a-second language training program started by his wife, Patricia Roven. Employees also have access to computer training, interest-free loans to buy PCs, nurse-consulting hotlines, and tutorials on investment planning.

As Optiva moves to increase its product line and to reduce its dependency on the Sonicare toothbrush, Giuliani plans to apply another lesson learned at Hewlett Packard. From HP founder Bill Hewlett, Giuliani learned the importance of not pinning a company to one product. He remembers a time at HP when one of the work teams wanted to stop work on developing a new electronic tool for engineers. Bill Hewlett overruled them, thus ensuring that the first handheld electric calculator was invented by HP.

Reflection: A Path of Perception

For Neil Braun and David Giuliani, reflection is a unique path of perception. Each man has examined his experiences by asking a litany of leading questions: What? Why? And now what?

Whether we consider Giuliani's lesson about homework or Braun's adoption of Frank Biondi's performance review, we can detail reflection as a kind of inductive logic.[5] In Giuliani's and Braun's reflections, they described a particular experience (what happened), explored its significance (why it had an impact), and applied it as a more general lesson (what to do in a similar experience).

As David Giuliani explains, this logic is enlivened by self-observation. "I have always liked to watch myself work and see what the cutting edge is for me, and put my effort into the parts of myself that I really want to burnish and grow. I keep myself almost like a little piece of sculpture, always being worked on. Some parts, I let dry; other parts, I keep my hand on and try to shape myself into what I want to be. It's a long, gradual process."

Like Giuliani, AtlantiCare CEO George Lynn and Emmy–winning producer Steve Cannell are leaders who watch themselves work and whose reflections mirror self-appraisal. Their habits of mind suggest what economist Adam Smith called "becoming the third eye."[6]

George Lynn, President and CEO, AtlantiCare Health System: The Conduct of Reflection

As president and CEO of AtlantiCare Health System, George Lynn has long been recognized as a leader and innovator in health care reform. His reflective style as a leader suggests the legacy of his education in a Catholic seminary, where he learned about "redemption as an individual act." Yet Lynn chooses the image of a conductor, rather than a pastor, as a guiding metaphor for observing his impact as a leader.

As he explains, "As a leader, you are trying to conduct the orchestra, trying to launch a process where everyone else can connect. When you finally bring yourself in, you are not playing any instruments. You have selected the music, interpreted it, and laid it out in a way that people can question it."

This image sets the stage for Lynn's self-observation: "I can study myself by noting whether people are reacting with harmony. Are they working collaboratively? Are they supporting each other? Are they working with a common purpose? If they are not, I am not providing the right kind of leadership, I have not picked the right music."

Even in times of discord, Lynn relies on self-reflection to guide his leadership. He recalls a painful public attack on his leadership during his tenure as president of the Atlantic City Medical Center and offers us a front-row seat to observe his conduct—his inner work—in a situation he describes as "having your pants pulled down in public."

The occasion for his reflection came during a bumpy financial quarter when the board overruled Lynn's protests and insisted on widespread layoffs at the Atlantic City Medical Center. It was a move that jolted the organization, creating a front-page story that revealed Lynn's salary and implied that his wife's job at the hospital feathered the family nest.

Lynn is wonderfully candid about the phases of his reflection. He explains, "The first thing that happens when you are attacked is that your defenses go up, and you say, 'I'm entitled to the money—I work hard—I went to school to get an MBA from Wharton!' But when you examine your defenses, they are meaningless. Because what you need to do is to become vulnerable and to make truthful relationships with people. People needed to know that I wasn't doing anything wrong."

And so Lynn gathered employees, medical staff, and board members and spoke to them from the podium. The memory is vivid: "It was the first time in my life that I talked to a group of people and couldn't get any saliva into my mouth." Lynn explained that his salary was set by the board and that his wife was a nurse practitioner who worked with AIDS patients. He then underlined his belief that he hadn't done anything wrong, except perhaps not fighting harder against the layoffs.

Lynn is convinced that his reflection and subsequent speech galvanized the organization's people. "They realized I was for real," he notes. "They saw me keep working through a personally embarrassing situation and not being torn apart. I learned that leaders can become accountable by being vulnerable. If you don't allow yourself to be vulnerable, you can't get respect."

A final example of how Lynn conducts his leadership through the mirror of reflection reveals that he uses self-appraisal as a test of his leadership. Listen to Lynn describe how he worked himself out of a job: "When I was president of Atlantic City Medical Center, I was the chief planner of a plan for an integrated health care system. As the plan crystallized, I realized that making it work would require me to quit my secure prestigious job as president to run this new system."

Upon reflection, Lynn understood, "I could convince the board that we could start to make this new plan work without me leaving my job, but I would be fooling them and fooling myself. So I recognized I had to give up the security of my job at the medical center and take on this integrated delivery system where the risks were greater than the rewards."

For Lynn, his reflection created a first—and critical—test of his own plan. He asked himself, "If I am not committed to it, how can I expect anyone else to be?"

Lynn's willingness to reflect on the consistency of his own behavior reminds us of a wonderful story about a woman who brought her young son to see India's great pacifist Mohandas Gandhi in the hope that he could convince her son to give up his addiction to chewing sugarcane. In the story, Gandhi listens to the mother's plea and asks her to return in three weeks. When the mother returns, Gandhi offers her son a boilerplate lecture about the evils of sugarcane. The mother then turns to Gandhi and asks, "Sir, why could you not have told my son these things three weeks ago?" And Gandhi replies, "Because, Madam, three weeks ago I chewed the sugar cane."

Similarly, Lynn's habit of mind of reflection is the source of his candid and crucial self-observation.

Stephen J. Cannell, President, Cannell Studios: Knowing "When to and When Not To"

Producer Stephen J. Cannell offers a succinct summary of reflection as a way of observing himself as a leader. As he puts it, "I make a lot of mistakes, but I am alert to them. When I catch myself behaving badly, the way I wasn't raised to behave, I drop a flag on myself. I get angry with myself; I know it's insecurity—a sign of weakness and not strength—and I say to myself, 'What's bothering you, Steve?' "

Whenever he catches himself doing what he calls "a Steve Cannell commercial," or "taking a swipe at somebody," Cannell stops and reflects about his behavior with a reminder: "This is telling me I am scared right now. Maybe my last couple of scripts didn't get the response I'm used to getting at the network. Maybe I'm worried these guys are talking me down behind my back." Then he acts to counter his reaction: "Instead of exhibiting egotism and insecurity, I'm going to shut up, work harder, and see if I can turn that around."

Still, Cannell recalls—with the off-color language of a Hollywood producer and best-selling novelist—a time he "behaved badly" and cost his company a series of lucrative contracts at ABC Television. "They hated it; it was like I had urinated on their floor," says Cannell, describing ABC's response to the first screening of a pilot he had produced. Yet when the show aired, it was fifth in the ratings that week and one of the highest-rated movies ever, leading ABC to call a meeting to discuss developing six more episodes.

When Cannell arrived at the meeting, an ABC executive told him that before the network would order the episodes, he needed to have a conversation with Cannell about how to make a good movie. As Cannell spins the scenario, "I'm biting my lip; I'm starting to lose it. I've got Emmys on my shelf, and here is this executive giving me a primer about how films are constructed."

Cannell lost control, saying, "You guys are solely responsible for what happened; you picked the cast, forced a director on me, and approved every draft of this script. I went into my own pocket for a million dollars to reshoot scenes. If you don't like the movie, look in the mirror; don't just look at me. Let's not talk about good filmmaking. You can either buy the show, or stick it up your a__. I couldn't care less." The executive deadpanned, "I guess the ball is in my court." Cannell's company didn't get another job at ABC for seven years.

Immediately afterward, Cannell appraised his behavior and applied a lesson in leadership. As he explains, "I was out of control. It was ungentlemanly, unfriendly, and uncalled-for behavior. I had been in television for twenty years, and I knew that producers have to take the heat for projects that are seen as not up to network standards. My emotions were hot, and it cost my company a lot of shows."

Upon reflection, here's what Cannell wishes he would have

said: "Look, we obviously have a difference of opinion, and rather than get into a long, contentious discussion, why don't I just take a pass on this project and catch you next time."

His lesson can be summed up by a piece of advice proffered by producer and actor Jack Webb, for whom he worked at Universal Studios. In his droll *Dragnet*-style monotone, Webb informed Cannell, "Hey, Pal-ey, you got to know when *to* and when *not* to."

Reflection: The Socratic Command

The reflections of George Lynn and Steve Cannell illustrate a variety of ways that leaders heed Socrates' imperative to "know thyself." As a habit of mind, this command has two components. First, reflection involves recognizing your internal state. For instance, Steve Cannell recognizes that a "Cannell commercial" signals his insecurity. Or consider George Lynn, who reads about his salary on the front page, and then examines and tears down his defenses. The jargon for this manner of reflection is *metacognition*, or an awareness of thought, and *metamood*, or an awareness of mood.

The second element of self-knowing is most critical to leaders. Lynn and Cannell glimpse not only themselves, but also the impact of their behavior on others. D. H. Lawrence called this knowledge "recognition of the other" and made it the centerpiece of his novels and poetry.[7] A leader's ability to appraise his or her impact on others separates reflection from introspection. Recall Harold Shapiro's reflections on the Princeton budget debacle and his recognition that he "wasn't sufficiently sensitive to people's losses." In this way, reflection becomes the busy intersection between the private and public.

How Reflection Creates Context

A final facet of reflection involves the way leaders examine their experience by placing people and events in a larger context. Ellen

Futter, president of the American Museum of Natural History in New York, has been called a "Jurassic Joan of Arc" for her crusade to modernize that venerable institution. Applying the lessons of experience has been critical to her success in mobilizing her staff to create a vibrant new museum in the context of its historic mission.

Ellen Futter, President, American Museum of Natural History: A Parallel Play

Barnard College president Ellen Futter had been the youngest college president in U.S. history when she accepted the top post at one of the oldest museums in the country.[8] The job description was daunting: to update, freshen, and modernize the museum best known for being home of the tallest freestanding dinosaur in the world. And, as Futter explains, "to give the museum a more visible role—to debunk the notion of science as a remote enterprise."

To understand the challenge Futter faced, recall Holden Caulfield, J. D. Salinger's infamous adolescent, who sought sanctuary in the American Museum of Natural History because "in that museum, everything stayed right where it was. You could go there a hundred thousand times and the deer would still be drinking out of that water hole."[9]

Futter is meeting this challenge of modernizing the museum for the millennium with a unique model of reflection that is inspired by her roles as president of Barnard College and as a parent of two young daughters. She artfully applies the lessons of her experience to understand the culture and context of the museum.

Futter's tenure at Barnard College was the earliest model for her ability to push an institution without having it push back. As Futter explains, "In my early years at Barnard, I developed a keen appreciation for process, a real understanding of the importance of the culture of the institution. It is more than a sense of being careful; it's being true to institutional values."

The lesson in leadership for Futter is clear: "Issuing edicts can make certain things happen, but it won't necessarily make them happen in an optimal way." Her application of this lesson in her leadership is just as crisp. In every discussion about change with an educator, scientist, or curator, Futter emphasizes the bigger picture: The context for making changes will remain within the traditional mission of the museum.

Futter's smart summary of her message: "The core holds." She elaborates, "In my discussion with educators and scientists, they don't hear a change in our basic mission of scientific research and education. We are not changing the museum's core activities and goals or bumping up against its historical underpinnings. To the contrary, everything we are doing to freshen and modernize is being done in light of the underlying mission."

Creating this context of continuity—keeping everyone's eye on the museum's mission—is one key to Futter's success as an agent of change. Another is how she applies a lesson from watching her young daughters play. Futter uses the guiding metaphor of "parallel play" to characterize the pitfall of solo missions among the museum's three groups of players: education, exhibition, and research.

In describing the meaning of her metaphor, she says, "Those of us who have small children know that when you invite a two or three year old over to play, one child plays with blocks and the other plays with three different toys. The parents are happy because their kids are 'playing,' even though they are not interacting very much. But when you have major departments engaged in parallel play, you just don't get the synergy or maximum-quality product."

Futter recalls, with great pleasure, the way the planning process for the Leonardo da Vinci–Codex Leicester Exhibition brought all three departments into play. Perhaps it was the challenging nature of the ancient manuscript—with its pages written backward in Italian—that united the group to wonder how it could bring this book to life.

Futter describes the scene: "Suddenly, the scientists are saying, 'You see that drawing in the upper left-hand corner? We have an example of that.' So suddenly we are bringing some collection into a manuscript exhibition. Then the educators are saying, 'We could take a piece of the exhibition space and build a room where people could try the experiments.' With the education, exhibition, and science departments working together this way, we created a very different kind of exhibition than we have had in the past."

Still, for all Futter's ability to reflect about past lessons in leadership, she was quite insistent that her self-observation must be a bonfire of vanities. "Leading is balancing," she says. "It's a delicate calibration of when you are leading, listening, or shaping. But I view it as ideas and programs. I am aware of my behavior, but I'm not selling me; I'm not the focal. To play with an idea is what the institutions I've been affiliated with are all about."

One final leader informs us. When John Bryan, CEO of Sara Lee, reflected on his behavior within the larger context of racism in America, he applied the lessons of his experience to create a lifelong commitment to diversity.

John Bryan, CEO, Sara Lee: "The Broad Sweep of History"

John Bryan's family and community in West Point, Mississippi, created many occasions for him to reflect about racism.[10] He describes his father, whose meatpacking company was the largest employer in town, as a man "without a racist bone in his body." He watched his social worker mother—"a dyed-in-the-wool Roosevelt Democrat"—work with handicapped, impoverished, and retarded citizens. He also recalls how she refused to accept her diploma from the University of Mississippi because it was signed by Governor Izzo Bilbo, whom Bryan termed "the most vile racist in the history of America."

While his parents were remarkably free of bigotry, Bryan had to initiate his own reflections about racism at an early age. He remembers an early moment of meaning: "My mother was raised on a traditional southern plantation with sixty black families. I grew up playing with black children, but when I was twelve, one of the maids told me to quit playing with the black children—because that was what you had to do. Then when I was eighteen, I joined Head Start and began to have strong questions about the way [blacks and whites] related."

In college, Bryan created a larger context for his reflections. He recalls, "I understood the early rumblings and quickly grasped the fact that racism didn't fit into the ethical models that I was studying. I developed an intellectual awareness of where we were in the sweep of history; I knew things were going to change. And I was not going to be identified with a racist view. If there was a chance for leadership, I would jump into it."

Bryan soon got the chance, when his father made him president of the family business at the ripe old age of twenty-four. With the clout that came from running the company, Bryan fought to end the town's long-standing segregation policies. As Bryan puts it, "I was the largest employer in town, and I had the responsibility to lead. So I went around and integrated. I tore down signs and integrated our company's facilities. I became president of the Chamber of Commerce and started trying to lead the town in a new direction. I was confronted with issues, and I had to make choices."

Bryan's choices as a leader reflect his determination to apply the lessons about his experience with racism. First, Bryan became head of the school board and sued the school district to require the integration of the schools. Then, in 1964, when the city council bulldozed the public swimming pool to avoid a federal order to integrate, Bryan borrowed $26,000 from a bank in Alabama to build a pool that African American residents could use.

Years later, after Bryan Foods was merged into Consolidated Foods, which, in turn, became Sara Lee, we see how CEO Bryan's legacy of reflecting about racism has become part of the company's policy. As he explains, "Many people haven't seen the kinds of horrors connected to discrimination that I saw in my youth. Because I have had these experiences, I got interested in diversity issues. We must start out by asking, What are we going to do about these issues in the company?"

Bryan summarizes how Sara Lee addresses diversity: "A vast majority of our resources—our foundation and programmatic work—goes toward minorities and social issues. We have been aggressive in our diversity programs, taking action and trying to move the numbers to create more opportunities for minorities and a more integrated workforce for us. We are trying for a higher percentage of minorities on our board." (Note: Seven of Sara Lee's twenty-eight board members are African American, women, or foreign nationals.)

How do Bryan's reflections about diversity relate to the company's bottom line? Bryan admits, "The business imperative will probably be the motivation for most companies. Social justice is not immediately obvious to those who grew up in another generation. A lot of my business friends say, 'What in the world is with you? You can't get involved in that!' " And Bryan answers with a striking self-appraisal that underlines his habit of mind: "I can't help it. I'm the issues person. I am my mother's son; I have to."

Reflection as Reorganization

Princeton president Harold Shapiro explains how reflection is a habit of mind that organizes experience. "Events are like theater. They capture your attention, but they don't form you as a person. And you only get formed as a person by contemplating that experience, trying to give your experience order and meaning."

The leaders we've described have examined their experience and given it "order and meaning" in several ways: appraising their own behavior, creating a context, and applying the lessons of experience. Although the faces of reflection are strikingly different—from Sara Lee's John Bryan viewing racism in the broad sweep of history, to NBC president Neil Braun's "Just in Case" journal; from Optiva CEO Giuliani's sloppy homework to Ellen Futter's remodeling the Great Hall of Dinosaurs—the results are similar.

Each leader used reflection as an act of making meaning, a unique insight that organized the present with an eye toward both the future and the past.[11] The habit of mind of reflection is the essence of Proust's observation on his search for the perfect Madeleine. "The voyage of discovery is not in seeking new landscapes," said Proust, "but in having new eyes."

NOTEBOOK: REFLECTION

After NBC president Neil Braun's experience teaching high school, he applied the lesson of the students' honesty and tolerance with his request for truth telling at staff meetings.

- Describe a family member or exemplar who provided a model of examining and then applying the lessons of experience.

- Identify a time when, like Neil Braun, you were moved by a powerful experience. What specific steps did you (or could you) take to incorporate this event as a lesson in your leadership?

AtlantiCare CEO George Lynn compares his self-observation to that of a conductor and studies his own leadership by noting whether people are working in harmony.

- Specify someone in your organization who draws upon reflection to appraise his or her impact on others. What key behaviors suggest this habit of mind is being employed?

- Describe a time when your "third eye" was critical to resolving a problem or when a resolution was stalled because of a failure to reflect. How do you (or could you) observe your behavior and its impact on others in your work setting?

President Ellen Futter met the challenge of modernizing the American Museum of Natural History by encouraging her staff to see the changes in the larger context of the museum's enduring mission.

- List the leaders and experiences in your life that have provided an example of keeping an eye on the big picture. How have you translated these examples in your leadership?

- Recall an experience of crisis or challenge where you were able to stand back and see the issues in a broader perspective. How did this reflection inform your capacity to manage the situation or meet the challenge?

Consider Princeton President Harold Shapiro's observation that events are like theater and that we can only develop as people by creating an order and meaning about events.

- Name an event that contributed to your development as a leader because of your reflection and the meaning you created about the experience.

Chapter 5

Framework

Creating an Optimistic Narrative

W hen Cherokee chief Wilma Mankiller was ten years old, her family moved from the wooded hills of Adair County, Oklahoma, to the city of San Francisco as part of the Bureau of Indian Affair's Relocation Program. "It was total culture shock," remembers Mankiller.[1] "One day we were living in a rural Cherokee community, growing strawberries, hauling water for plumbing, bartering with neighbors, and listening to the sounds of coyotes and owls. A few days later, we were living in California, trying to deal with the mysteries of television, neon lights, and elevators, listening to the sounds of traffic and police sirens."

As Mankiller watched her father respond to this cataclysmic change, she had her first glimpse of an *explanatory style* the Cherokee call "being of good mind." She describes this mental habit as a means of "thinking positively, taking what is handed out, and turning it into a better path."

She recalls her father's resilient framework: "My father took a situation that was devastating to our family—moving from a rural, isolated, insulated Cherokee community to one of the largest and most sophisticated cities in the world—and tried to help us see it in the most positive way. He didn't dwell on the fact that we had left everything we had ever known. Instead, he focused on the positive things about San Francisco: the indoor plumbing, central heating and electricity, the better educational system, and the opportunity for jobs."

Chief Mankiller has translated the legacy of her father's example of "the Cherokee way" into an optimistic framework that guides her stewardship of the Cherokee Nation. In this chapter, we detail how Mankiller and other leaders draw upon framework as a habit of mind that creates a positive explanatory style.[2] This inner narrative of framework translates into powerful acts of leadership.

"Being of Good Mind"

Mankiller explains that many traditional Cherokee prayers start with a plea for a positive framework. The medicine man or spiritual leader often begins a prayer by asking participants to remove all negative thoughts from their minds. "It is impossible to focus on the subject matter if negative thoughts are running around," says Mankiller. "Being of good mind means that you don't allow your thinking to be controlled by negative thoughts." She believes that the connection between thought and deed determines how people behave. She explains, "The literal translation (of the Cherokee word) means being on a good path."

For Mankiller, a moment of meaning with a medicine man crystallized her commitment to this distinctly Cherokee framework. Mankiller sets the scene: "When I was in my thirties, I was an up-and-coming person at the Cherokee Nation. There was a woman with close ties to the chief who always seemed to put roadblocks in my way. I intensely disliked her—and I didn't like the feeling—so I went to see a medicine man."

Mankiller arrived at sunrise. For the next six hours, they sang, drank tea, and talked. By noon, she had a different and more positive explanation for this negative situation. She recalls, "By then, whatever negative feeling of dislike I had toward this woman were gone, and I began to see her as my sister, as someone who had a problem. I understood that it wasn't me; but something within her that caused her to react to me in a particular way."

For Mankiller, this event of knowing gave a name to her father's framework and the explanatory style she had observed over many years. "From the medicine man, I learned that our culture had a way of resolving negative feelings—that being of good mind was the Cherokee way," she says. Her discovery was the beginning of a framework that has organized her experience as a leader in the decades that followed.

Mankiller sums up this habit of mind: "Try to keep your mind free of negative thoughts. When you encounter a difficult person or situation, you have a choice about whether to focus on the negative attributes or seeing the connection to a larger universe and trying to find something positive. Sometimes the only positive approach is asking, 'What did I learn?' "

From the rich legacy found in "being of good mind," Mankiller carries several lessons that are key elements of the inner resource of framework: choosing a positive focus, creating an optimistic explanatory style, and achieving mastery by reframing. Three examples illustrate how this kind of inner narrative became a framework to shape Mankiller's unique path as a leader.

The Bell Project: Choosing a Positive Focus

As director of the Cherokee Nation Community Development Department in the early 1980s, Wilma Mankiller led the tribe's most daunting project: the revitalization of the troubled, impoverished community of Bell in eastern Oklahoma. Many of the surrounding communities had predicted the failure of this project, but Mankiller's framework allowed her to lead the people of Bell to success.

"It was a classic case of looking at the community and seeing something totally different than what everybody else saw," Mankiller says. "Everyone looked at Bell and saw people hauling water for plumbing, young students dropping out of school, families moving away, schools in danger of closing, neighbors settling disputes with violence."

Mankiller framed Bell's prospects with a more positive focus. She recalls, "I used the concept of being of good mind here. When I looked at the same community, I saw they had a strong sense of culture and interdependence. Families shared the few resources they had; 95 percent of the people still spoke Cherokee. I knew we had a choice of either focusing on the negative—wringing our hands and saying this is hopeless—or asking, What are the positives here?"

The positives prevailed, and the success of the Bell project has been widely reported. Bell residents laid a sixteen-mile pipeline that carried water into many homes for the first time, remodeled dilapidated housing, and constructed new homes. It became a model of Native American self-sufficiency.

Mankiller's success in shepherding the citizens of Bell caught the eye of Ross Swimmer, then principal chief of the Cherokee Nation. He encouraged her to run on his ticket as deputy chief. In her campaigns and her terms in office, Mankiller's ability to choose a positive focus—to be of good mind—ripened into an optimistic explanatory style that is a hallmark of her leadership.

Getting Out the Vote: Creating an Explanatory Style

Mankiller's candidacy tested her framework of being of good mind. "To say that my campaign for deputy chief was heated would be the understatement of all time," says Mankiller. Those who did not want a woman in office sent her hate mail, slashed her tires, harassed her on the phone, and sent death threats. One disturbing memory stands out. Mankiller was riding in a parade when she saw a young man pointing and firing an imaginary pistol in her direction.

Mankiller relies on her inner narrative to explain this ugly encounter: "I told myself that he had a right to dissent, that he was only one person out of the 2,500 people I passed in the parade. And most of those people were supportive. But as I had learned in the situation I brought to the medicine man, when this man pointed a gun, it was more reflective of something that was wrong with him than something wrong with me."

Mankiller was clear about her framework for the campaign. As she puts it, "I built my run for office on a positive and cheerful foundation to counter the incredible hostility I encountered." Her bottom line: "I said to myself, 'Okay, if I let these people siphon off my energy debating silly issues like whether or not a woman should be elected chief, I'm going to lose the election.' "

Changing Two Minds:
Achieving Mastery by Reframing

Mankiller won the election. When Swimmer resigned from office to run the Bureau of Indian Affairs, she became principal chief—a position to which she was reelected with 83 percent of the vote. During her tenure as principal chief, tribal membership tripled in size, the annual budget doubled, and a vast array of innovative services and programs were initiated, including the construction of an $11 million youth and job corps training center.

For Mankiller, this center was built by being of good mind. "The job center was not a popular program. The tribal council voted nine to seven against it," remembers Mankiller. "If I didn't have this idea of being of good mind, I would have given up. But instead, I thought, 'All I need to do is to go back and try to change the minds of just two people on the council.'"

She got them to change their minds, and the center was built. Chief Mankiller sums up the way reframing allowed her to master this and other difficult situations. "Never, never give up. Leaders don't say, 'Oh my God, there is a barrier; I'm going home.' They would rather look at a barrier and see it as a challenge, saying, 'If I can't go over it, can I go around it? Can I go under it? Can I move it?' That's the way most leaders I know do things."

The Meaning of Framework

From her rich legacy of "the Cherokee way," Chief Mankiller has transformed framework into a habit of mind that enriches her leadership. Her success in the Bell community was powered by her choice of a positive focus. In the heat of the election campaign, she created an optimistic explanatory style with an inner narrative that avoided taking the blame for negative attacks or blowing them out of proportion. Mankiller was also able to achieve mastery by reframing the tribal council's veto of the vocation center. Instead of accepting defeat, she reframed the situation as a two-vote deficit.

Mankiller's resilience and optimism allow us to understand framework as a habit of mind that creates a distinct kind of meaning in the life and work of leaders. But an optimistic framework does not include the following: a pixilated leader whistling a happy tune, a Rodgers and Hammerstein heroine christening herself a "cockeyed optimist," or Norman Vincent Peale's "power of positive thinking" recycled for the new millennium.

Instead, an optimistic framework is a powerful scheme of meaning.[3] As Chief Mankiller suggests, it is a habit of mind in which positive thoughts and words (inner narrative) are directly linked to deeds (of mastery). Thus, framework is found not only in the way leaders report and explain their experience, it also becomes a means of acting upon their experience.

This outline of framework is also evident in the leadership of Brenda Lauderback, whose choice of a positive focus is a powerful dimension of her leadership.

Brenda Lauderback, Group President, Nine West: "The Only Limits Are in Your Mind"

Early in her career, Brenda Lauderback, group president of Nine West, employed a positive framework to pave her path to leadership. Lauderback remembers her resilient response to the discouraging words of the president of Dayton Hudson Company following her promotion to buyer in women's sportswear.

As Lauderback recalls, "He came to congratulate me. I shared my career goal of becoming vice president and general merchandising manager (GMM). He looked at me and said, 'Maybe you shouldn't set your goals too high. You will probably be disappointed. In the history of the company, there has never been a Jewish, or female, much less black, vice president and GMM.' "

Lauderback describes her *inner narrative*: "What he said was true, and he was only trying to help. But what he said energized me, and I thought, 'You're right; it's about time. I'm going to position myself. Somebody has to be the first and it might as well be me.' " These optimistic thoughts were then linked to her words and deeds.

First she told the paternal president, "In time, things will change, and I will be the first." Then Lauderback continued to gain promotions within the company until she became the first female, the first African American, and the youngest person to become a vice president and GMM in the company.[4] She explained her clear lesson in leadership: "I learned that no matter what the intention, you can never let anybody put limits on you. The only limitations you have are in your own mind."

Lauderback's on-the-job training also echoes the legacy of her mother's leadership: "My mother ran her own business and marched to a different drummer. I remember her coming to school to talk to a teacher who was encouraging the girls in my class to prepare themselves to be secretaries. 'Why limit their dreams?' she asked him. Mother believed that there was nothing you couldn't accomplish, but that you had to figure out the strategies to get it done."

When it came to framing setbacks and negative events, Mother knew best. As Lauderback explains, "She believed that once you have a vision and something goes wrong, you have to pick yourself up, brush yourself off, and reassess the situation so you can go about meeting your goal in a different way." She gave Lauderback a template for choosing a positive focus by telling her, "If you reach for the stars and fall short, don't think about how you have fallen short, think about how far you have reached."

Lauderback transforms and communicates this resilient habit of mind in her leadership at Nine West. "I try to communicate to my people the idea that what you think and what you believe determines what you can accomplish," she says. Whether her staff is minding a merger or pressured to turn out a product in record time, Lauderback chooses a positive focus. "When we have a problem, we figure it out by clarifying and strategizing and pooling our talents and resources," she says. "There is never the thought that we can't turn it around."

Lauderback uses her leadership to set an example of positive framework and to pass on the lessons of mastery she has learned. As she puts it, "We all have to work with a variety of people, and everyone has their own baggage, their own interpretation. We have to grasp the positive note if we want to control and change our reality."

Inner Narrative: Composing the Event

Like Chief Mankiller, Brenda Lauderback's leadership is guided by a powerful inner narrative, one that allows her to explain and master challenging negative situations by relabeling them. The positive frameworks of these two leaders point to what psychologist Robert Kegan has described as "the zone between an event and a reaction to it."[5]

Applying Kegan's view, framework is the "place where an event is privately composed—where it actually *becomes* an event for the person." In Lauderback's reaction to the event with the patronizing president or Chief Mankiller's response to the threatening gesture in the parade, each leader's private composition creates their inner narrative.

To understand how this private composition is expressed in an inner narrative, we ask you to pick an airport and picture yourself on a delayed flight parked on the runway. Imagine that your fearless flight crew has just announced a negative event: Departure is postponed an additional forty-five minutes. Then listen to your seatmates give voice to their inner narratives.

Your neighbor to the left winces, checks his watch, and mutters, "If this doesn't take off soon, I'm going to miss my meeting and blow this deal out of the water! Why did I fly out on a Friday? I should have known better."

To your right comes the less negative, more masterful narrative: "If this doesn't take off soon, I'll call the gang in Chicago and push the meeting forward. Fridays are a real madhouse. I'll sure be glad when this flight is over."

The resilient leaders we have studied and worked with would respond to this delayed plane, or a dip on Wall Street, or a board member chewing the scenery with their signature style in composing an optimistic inner narrative. Psychologist Martin Seligman calls this an "explanatory style." And Bill Shore, founder and executive director of the nation's largest antihunger organization, Share Our Strength, offers a front-row seat to watch how an optimistic explanatory style shapes his leadership.

Bill Shore, Founder and Executive Director, Share Our Strength: Taking the Long View

Share Our Strength (SOS) executive director Bill Shore traces his optimistic framework to forays with his father, who ran the local office of Pittsburgh congressman Bill Moorhead in the 1950s. A trip to the pizza parlor could take more than an hour because people would stop his father to ask him about getting an uncle into the veteran's hospital, finding a lost Social Security check, or checking on a fiancé's immigration papers. As the pizza grew cold, eight-year-old Shore would tug on his father's sleeve and observe his explanations.

As Shore remembers, "Whatever the problem, he had seen it before. He was the doctor who knew the fever would come down, the shopkeeper who could order more. He would say, 'Don't worry. It should work out. Call me Monday, at the office.' He never had a lofty philosophy of life, but he had a rule for navigating the icy streets of Pittsburgh in winter, and they may have been one and the same: You can get anywhere you want to go if you just take your time."[6]

Years later, when Shore navigated the slippery streets of Washington, D.C., and New Hampshire on the senatorial and presidential campaign staffs of Colorado senator Gary Hart, he discovered that Hart and his father were, as he puts it, "two cards from the same deck." He elaborates, "My father always used to say that everything works out in the end. And Gary Hart used to take me aside and say, 'Nothing is as important as it seems at the time.' Hart had a strong sense that the ups and downs are transitory, and the real question was whether you were moving in the right direction. I internalized those two pieces of advice. It is part of my operating style at SOS to take the long view—not to overreact—to convey the sense that this, too, will pass."

What Shore describes as his "operating style" is also his explanatory style, or a distinct inner narrative that interprets (composes) negative events in a way that allows him to master them. As he explains, "If a grant gets turned down, a corporate partnership ends, or I have a disagreement with a board member, my inner voice says, 'Slow down, wait, take a look at this from several different sides before you act.' I try to take a long view in terms of what we want and how we can achieve that."

Shore used this explanatory style to deconstruct a recent cash flow deficit. "For the first time in fifteen years, we had an operating deficit of $1.2 million, and people were freaking out," says Shore. He took the long view and told them, "If your objective is to resolve this in sixty days, you have a good reason to freak out. But if you accept that we can't fix this immediately, then we can get ourselves on a glide path with a plan to phase this out over time. If we can manage with mileposts, this can become a relatively benign exercise."

Shore's clarity about the importance of a positive framework is reminiscent of Chicago Cubs president Andy MacPhail and his sandwich story. "I think most stress is artificially imposed on oneself," says Shore, "because the rest of the world looks the same five minutes from now as it did five minutes ago, and the only thing that is different is what is going on inside your head."

For Shore, this framework offers a different view of failure. As a leader, he avoids self-blame by reminding himself to ask: What can I learn from this? Although he recognizes the potential of failure to prevent future risk taking, he observes, "the lasting impact of failure is pretty short compared to the lasting impact of learning something from it."

Shore puts this perspective in practice in his leadership by creating a working environment at SOS where risk is rewarded and people are encouraged to take chances. If people beat themselves up over a mistake, Shore invites them to "be agile and move on," to take the long view, and to consider what they "did accomplish and what was learned for the future."

Perhaps the ultimate test of Shore's optimistic explanatory style was finding a hopeful way to frame the potential frustration of leading a worldwide antihunger organization—of coping with problems that appear to be endless. Shore chose the guiding metaphor of cathedral building to compose his positive perspective.

"When you walk around the planet," Shore says, "and try to find things that have been around for a thousand years, the cathedrals are it. I have used the metaphor of cathedral building to guide me in the process of working on something for my whole life that I will never see finished. I try to remember that builders of cathedrals didn't allow the fact that they would not see their work finished to detract from their craftsmanship and dedication. It actually enhanced it." For Shore, cathedral building provides an image of how to create social change that endures.

Studying Explanatory Style

Bill Shore demonstrates that changing the things you say to yourself when you experience setbacks or stressful events is the central skill of framework.[7] Whether he is coping with the loss of a corporate sponsor, dealing with a budget deficit, or confronting the enormous challenge of fighting worldwide hunger, Shore employs a positive inner narrative to relabel the situation and set the stage for mastering the problem at hand.

This marked ability of leaders to relabel stressful situations, as a means of mastery, was one of our first observations as psychologists in the field. In the early days of consulting with CEOs, we insisted on asking them to name their biggest stresses. With great consistency, leader after leader would tell us, "I'm not stressed, I'm challenged." Or "I'm excited!" At first, we suspected denial. Then we began to see the first outlines of optimistic framework. We learned that these leaders were displaying a habit of mind that allowed them to explain negative events in a masterful manner.

No one is more adept in describing the way an explanatory style leads to mastery than psychologist Martin Seligman. To understand why Seligman is the Godfather of framework, we have to travel back to the less politically correct 1960s when Seligman—like all good psychologists—was doing animal research. He was a graduate student who had arrived at Richard Solomon's laboratory at the University of Pennsylvania in the midst of a series of experiments that exposed dogs to high-pitched sounds and brief shocks.[8]

Seligman was stunned by how rapidly the dogs abandoned their attempts to escape the shocks and sat passively. He then devoted most of his career to explaining why. "It would take me ten years to prove to the scientific community that what afflicted those dogs was helplessness and that helplessness could be learned, and therefore, *unlearned* by teaching the animals that their actions could change their situation," wrote Seligman.[9]

Seligman immediately recognized the application of these experiments for humans. He felt that if we could cure an animal's helplessness by teaching them that their actions—namely, avoiding the shocks—had an effect, surely we could prevent helplessness in people by providing a similar experience of mastery. This mastery, Seligman believed, would be the result of developing an optimistic explanation style, which he defines as "a habitual, optimistic way to explain to yourself why things happen."

According to Seligman, there are three dimensions to explanatory style: permanence, pervasiveness, and personalization. When something goes awry and we try to explain it, for example, we always ask, How long will it last? How much of my life will be affected? Who is to blame?

When a person uses a pessimistic, or helpless, explanatory style, they explain negative events as being never-ending, ruinous, and all their fault. By contrast, leaders who employ an optimistic explanatory style view Maalox moments as temporary setbacks. Recall, for example, Bill Shore taking the long view on reducing SOS's budget deficit. These leaders confine the problem to a specific circumstance, such as when Chief Mankiller chose to view her threatening parade heckler as only one person in a crowd of 2,500. They also take realistic responsibility, such as Mankiller's lobbying to change a vote, rather than blame themselves and thus learn valuable lessons from their mistakes.

The role of a masterful explanatory style can be further explored in the experiences of Phyllis Campbell, a leader whose optimistic framework suggests her legacy of living in a Japanese-American family and of working in an industry where change is a career-long curriculum.

Phyllis Campbell, President, U.S. Bank of Washington: Reflection and Reframing

Phyllis Campbell, president of the U.S. Bank of Washington, is a third-generation Japanese American whose grandfather, Tamotsu Takisaki, was interned in World War II. She is also a cancer survivor and a navigator through numerous mergers and acquisitions. Campbell offers a succinct summary of her explanatory style: "With any adversity in life, it is not so much what happens to you as it is how you handle it."

Campbell "handles" adversity with an optimistic framework, one that results from her capacity to reflect and profit from her experiences. By transforming several elements of her legacy, she learned to create mastery by reframing challenging situations.

Her grandfather's legacy, after his return from an internment camp in Missoula, Montana, was the family's determination to avoid bitterness.[10] "My grandfather would say, 'This is my country, so if we had to be interned, then *shikata ga nai*,' which means things happen and you must accept your fate," remembers Campbell.

Campbell's inner work allows her to draw upon the wisdom of this cultural lesson—without adopting a powerless position. "The expression *shikata ga nai* became a filter," says Campbell. "For me, accepting your fate means accepting the things you cannot change and figuring out a way to move through them in a positive way. But if there is injustice, you must challenge it and accept your fate only when there has been a fair hearing."

The legacy of Campbell's twenty-five years with the U.S. Bank of Washington is her experiences of managing two mergers, presiding over the closing of dozens of branch banks, and sitting in the buyer's and the seller's chair in countless bank acquisitions. "The first one was the hardest, because I was a young officer. But the learning curve has gotten less steep every time," says Campbell. "By now, whenever there is an unexpected change, I can recognize the predictable emotional cycle of shock and dismay and talk myself through it."

Campbell's inner narrative reflects her adoption of *shikata ga nai* as well as the legacy of coping with change at the bank. When confronted with a challenge or sudden change, she employs a unique explanatory style that avoids self-blame or viewing adversity as permanent or ruinous. She says, "My dialogue is this: 'All right, it wasn't something you created or wanted to happen. It isn't in your control. But you have a choice to stay where you are, or deal with it and come out the other end a winner.' "

For Campbell, the next step is coaching her people to compose the events of change with this optimistic framework. "As a leader during a time of change, I think it is my obligation to first quickly deal with my own predictable emotional cycle," says Campbell. "Then it's my job to help people move through their feelings and to understand that we are all totally in control of how we react to major changes that we don't agree with or didn't engineer."

Campbell's capacity to reflect on her experiences, both in her family and the continuum of changes in banking, has shaped her fearless framework as a leader. As she puts it, "I've never been afraid of hard work. I'm willing to take on any challenge. And when I make mistakes, which is fairly often, I pick myself up and keep going."

For Campbell, every challenge or change brings an opportunity for new learning and taking responsibility. Campbell says, "I ask myself at the end of each process, 'What could happen better next time?' I tell myself, 'Don't be a victim; don't blame yourself for what didn't go right. Just don't do it that way next time.' "

Theories of Relativity

Each description of the inner narrative of framework is as unique as the leader who composes it. Still, all of these narratives share a common characteristic: Every leader's framework explains challenging events by putting them in perspective. Their framework becomes a theory of relativity. It is an explanatory style put into frequent practice when leaders master negative situations by relabeling them.

Many leaders use shorthand. They avoid viewing trouble as permanent and pervasive—or punishing themselves—by using a snapshot of a past moment of meaning or repeating a seed sentence. For example, Harry Kamen, chairman of the board and CEO of Metropolitan Life Insurance, woke up on the first morning of his vacation to find the story about a fraud investigation of MetLife's Florida offices on the front page of the *Wall Street Journal*.

Kamen explains how he interpreted this catastrophic publicity and the investigation that followed by offering his theory of relativity. "My mother had left her whole family in Europe during the war; she used to write to them every month. I remember the day she received a whole package of letters back and realized they had all been killed. *That* was a catastrophe; this was not," Kamen says.

Ellen Bravo, codirector of 9 to 5, the National Association of Working Women, describes several routes to relativity. The first, and fastest, is a seed sentence that grew in response to her fears about speaking at the public forums that defined politics in the 1960s. As Bravo recalls, "I did my first real public speaking in Cleveland in the summer of 1966 at the Saturday morning soapboxes in the park. The first few times, I was so afraid of making mistakes."

But as Bravo continued to use the soapbox, her inner narrative changed. She began to tell herself, "You have the information that people need to make a difference. So you can't be thinking about yourself and how nervous you are." She passes this lesson on to those employees and members who fear trying. To create a positive perspective about speaking up, Bravo tells them, "Remember that you have the goods people need. So focus on the experience and information you have. People will be better off when you are done."

Bravo's explanatory style is characterized by a habit of mind that places problems in a relative perspective. She says, "I have a litany of questions I ask myself: Will the world come to an end? If I had cancer would I care about this? If I had a best friend who was blaming herself for this situation, what would I say to her? Or what if my kids asked me, 'Mom, is it really such a big deal?' "

For Bravo, any setback is buffered by "knowing how to count." As she explains, "I count special things at the same time I count problems. I count the people I collaborate with and remind myself there are other people who wake up and worry in the middle of the night. And I count victories. Every person who feels more powerful makes one more step toward the life they want to live."

Our description of framework as a positive perspective will be complete with the story of a local hero. He is John Stanford, the optimistic and ebullient superintendent of Seattle's public schools who, it has been said, "almost single-handedly made people believe in the power of public education again."[11] Stanford died of acute myelogenous leukemia as we were writing this chapter.

John Stanford, Superintendent, Seattle Public Schools: "Victory Is in the Classroom"

For John Stanford, superintendent of Seattle public schools, his family and community provided his education as an optimist. He says, "I grew up in a little town I now refer to as Camelot. It was on the black side of a town called Yeadon, Pennsylvania. And in Camelot, there were no fights, no girls got pregnant, no boys went to jail, everybody graduated from school, and everyone supported each other. It was a place where people loved me and viewed me with spirit. People have always directed positive things to me."

Stanford describes his family template: "My father was a very, very positive person. He worked at two or three jobs, and he was always building, thinking about how to do things better. He always had a pad of paper with him, figuring out how to make ends meet.

My mother was full of energy—a dancer, a risk taker, a poker player. My parents both taught themselves to read. And because they never discouraged me, even when things didn't go well, I grew up believing in taking chances."

Stanford remembers several moments of meaning that fueled his optimistic framework. He recalls the fiasco of trying to fix the front door because his parents couldn't afford the cost of a locksmith. "I took it apart, but never did get it back together again," he admits. "It cost them even more money to finally get it fixed. But instead of being angry with me, they encouraged me for trying to fix it."

His parents' reframing of his failure emboldened Stanford, at age 14, to borrow a neighbor's wheelbarrow, to order several yards of cement, and to pour a concrete floor underneath the house. "That really surprised my dad," says Stanford. "But my parents had given me the feeling that I could do anything and that I could accomplish anything with others."

Years later, as a two-star general without any prior experience as an educator, Stanford translated and employed this optimistic framework to meet the challenge of becoming Seattle's superintendent of public instruction. In the early days of his leadership, he revealed the resilient inner narrative that allowed him to reframe any cynicism about his potential for success. Stanford recalls a national superintendents' forum where a colleague told him, "John, you need to know that they hired you to fire you; so you better look for a place to fall. The other superintendents just won't accept you."

Consider how Stanford's inner narrative created the framework for his future success. First, he did not personalize the threat. He said, "They hired me to fire me? That says more about those people than it says about me. And if they resent me, that's their problem. I believe they hired me to get the job done, and I am going to get it done." Then he contained the damage by refusing to see the problem as permanent or pervasive. He also reframed his job in a masterful way, saying, "I'm not looking for a place to fall; I'm looking for a place to lift up this district and these children. I'm here for the children."

Stanford also refused to see being fired as a catastrophe. "If they fire me, it is going to be for pushing too hard or moving too fast. I don't care if they fire me; I will find something else to do. I must be bold for these children," insisted Stanford. And in talking to Roger Erskine, executive director of the Seattle Education Association, we learned of a wonderful example of how Stanford's optimism allowed him to be bold.[12]

When John Stanford began his tenure as Seattle's superintendent of public schools, he scheduled a weekly two-hour meeting with Roger Erskine. Here, the two shared their dreams about improving the quality of the student-teacher relationships in a school district preoccupied with such "adult problems" as class size, teacher-principal conflict, and department heads competing for dwindling dollars.

Then one day, with his signature explanatory style, Stanford reframed the situation in terms of a solution rather than the problem. Calling Erskine on the phone, he told him he had created a new phrase to capture the essence of their shared belief of giving top priority to the student-teacher relationship. Using a guiding metaphor from the military, he told Erskine, "Victory is in the classroom!"

As Roger Erskine recalls, "That was probably my best day ever. John and I were both optimists; so rather than focusing on the problems, we wanted to give teachers a picture of what a solution should look like. By saying 'Victory is in the classroom,' we were putting the focus onto the classroom and not on administration. Reframing the issue this way became a rallying point—an opportunity for people to set aside their beliefs (about administrative problems) and look at the needs of the kids again."

The results of putting this metaphor in motion included principals and teachers collaborating on an academic achievement plan, a contract with a "trust agreement" for teachers, school budgets and staffing weighted toward student needs, and staff vacancies filled according to student needs.

In the third year of John Stanford's leadership—when parents stopped to shake his hand on the street and he received generally high marks for boosting test scores, enrollment numbers, public support, and record private donations to the schools—he was diagnosed with acute leukemia.[13] He met this challenge with a graceful and optimistic inner narrative. "I'm not angry and bitter," he said. "I'm not saying, 'Why me, God?' I'm saying, 'I have this illness, and I can defeat it.' "

Here is Stanford reframing his first round of chemotherapy: "Life is chemical and mental. When you are in the hospital, you've got these chemicals coursing through your body. But it's the mental part that drives you to be who you are and who you are going to be." And when Stanford returned to work two days after being released from the hospital, he said, "I'm not going to make any major changes in my life. I'm going to focus on living. If the disease wins, it wins. In the meantime, I'm going to continue to work and do things for others as long as I possibly can."

So Stanford worked during eight grueling months of unsuccessful treatments, which included a second course of chemotherapy, radiation, and a bone marrow transplant. Several weeks before he died, he told Don Neilson, vice president of the school board, "I want you to know that I am not quitting. I don't want to quit, I don't want my family to quit, and I don't want the kids to quit."

Each of the 3,000 people who attended John Stanford's memorial service are certain that the kids won't quit. At a Seattle service that preceded General Stanford's burial at Arlington National Cemetery, the program was filled with vintage Stanford quotes that reflect his resilient habits of mind, such as "Victory is in the classroom" and "Never give up, never give up, never give up!"

The students who spoke at the service suggest that Stanford's legacy of optimism will continue to energize parents, teachers, and students. In the words of twelve-year-old Mutandaa Kwwesele, a seventh grader at Seattle's Madison Middle School, we see the future of Stanford's optimistic framework: "We love you, John Stanford; your dreams are our dreams. . . . Let's warm this city and this nation with the kind of love and hope that we can call 'the Stanford hope.' Superintendent Stanford, your dream is a rocket. Let's ride."

The World of Yes

"Yes is a world," wrote the pithy poet e. e. cummings. "And in this world lies (skillfully curled) all other worlds."[14] Leaders whose framework organizes their leadership find many ways to say yes: Chief Wilma Mankiller saw the potential of the beleaguered town of Bell, Phyllis Campbell climbed the steep learning curve of corporate change, Bill Shore defied the budget deficit, and John Stanford found victory in the classroom.

These affirmative actions underline the idea that leadership is not a role, but a point of view. Each leader makes a deliberate choice to compose an inner narrative that puts negative events in a positive and relative perspective. These acts of reframing create meaning, mastery, and the opportunity to learn from mistakes.

When leaders choose to live in the world of yes, they can turn adversity into an event of knowing. They can map their work with teachable moments.

NOTEBOOK: FRAMEWORK

Cherokee chief Wilma Mankiller drew upon the Cherokee model for "being of good mind" in the successful revitalization of the impoverished community of Bell and in lobbying the tribal council to fund a youth and job corps training center.

- Identify a family member or exemplar who mastered challenging situations with a deliberate choice of a positive focus. How do you (or could you) apply his or her example in your approach to challenges in your leadership?

- Describe a situation in your organization where you face an uphill struggle. How could being of good mind—and choosing a positive framework—provide an inner resource for interpreting and managing the situation?

SOS executive director Bill Shore translated his father's resilient framework and that of Senator Gary Hart into an explanatory style that allows him to interpret negative events, such as facing a budget shortfall, by "taking the long view."

- Describe someone in your organization who interprets frustrating, disappointing outcomes with an optimistic, masterful explanatory style. What specific behaviors indicate this habit of mind at work?

- Recall a time when "taking the long view" (and viewing a difficult situation as temporary or specific) allowed you to respond in a resilient way. What current situations in your leadership might benefit from a similar approach?

MetLife CEO Harry Kamen puts events in relative perspective by remembering the genuine catastrophe of his mother losing her family. Ellen Bravo, codirector of 9 to 5, avoids catastrophic thinking by counting victories along with problems.

- Identify people or experiences in your life that have offered you a similar theory of relativity. Where in your leadership can you apply this habit of mind of putting challenging events in a relative perspective?

Explore Martin Seligman's idea that changing what you say to yourself in a negative situation is the central skill of framework.

(continued)

- Detail a recent setback or disappointment in two ways: first, as a permanent and pervasive situation; then, as a temporary and specific situation.

- What patterns do you see in comparing the two explanatory models? How can you apply this difference in your habit of mind in thinking about negative situations?

Chapter 6

Attunement

Learning from Those You Lead

W
e can't think of a better example of attunement—that habit of mind driven by learning from the people you lead—than Dr. Mitchell Rabkin's first official decision as CEO of Beth Israel Hospital in Boston: He abolished the doctors' dining room. His action telegraphed his desire for doctors to stay attuned to patients and fellow hospital employees. It also underlined his high regard for patients and staff.

Then, having toppled the hamburger hierarchy that is typical in many health care cafeterias, he created name badges that were the same for every employee, from physician to housekeeper. Rabkin's symbolic acts suggest one of the keys to the inner resource of attunement: regard for each individual's contribution. As Rabkin explains, "I wanted to convey my belief that everyone has an important role in the hospital."

Dr. Rabkin, now CEO of the Care Group, which includes the Harvard teaching hospital, Beth Israel, describes attunement as an inner resource that organizes his regard for individuals into a habit of mind.[1] By detailing the elements of this attunement, we illuminate this resource in the work of numerous leaders.

Regard for Each Individual

Mitchell Rabkin's attunement evolved from his ability to translate the impact of exemplars and moments of meaning throughout his career. He recalls the motivating model of an exemplar in medical school, Dr. Walter Bauer, who burned with a "clear blue light," showed exquisite sensitivity to patients, and insisted on telling them the truth. Rabkin also relates an illuminating moment, sparked by a story his wife, Adrienne, told him when she was a graduate student in social work.

Rabkin explains, "Adrienne commented to me about how much she admired a particular psychiatrist at the hospital. Whenever she observed him in the hospital's coffee shop, it was impossible to tell by his 'English' language whether he was talking to another physician, a patient's family, student, or employee. Everyone was dealt with in the same way. The story impressed me: his sense of the fundamental quality and humanity of everyone, regardless of their assigned role. After hearing this story, considering everyone of equal worth became a very important thing to me."

Over the years, Rabkin has integrated the legacy of these lessons about attunement into a habit of mind that creates meaning and shapes his actions as a leader. Rabkin's understanding and regard for the richness of each individual's experience is reflected in his directives, small and large. For instance, Beth Israel Hospital's in-house television station features employees from the laundry room or transportation saying, "You are watching WBIH Channel 3. Be well." Rabkin says, "I like these spots, because you get the sense of the many different people who make up the hospital." And Rabkin consistently delegates decision making to "the lowest possible level" of the hospital organization. He explains, "Regardless of your job, the quality of your work should be defined by the decisions you make."

Rabkin teaches what he practices. In his innovative freshman orientation for first-year medical students, Rabkin requires that they spend their first three days in the hospital wearing a nonmedical uniform and trying to do the job of someone in social services, housekeeping, or laundry. Rabkin is clear about the goals of this curriculum in attunement: "If your first contact with the hospital is as a medical student with a white coat and stethoscope, you already have the mantle of the doctor, and it distorts your view of how the place really works."

The result, Rabkin believes, is that doctors fail to see the importance of each employee and don't understand that life goes on when they are not there. Rabkin chuckles as he remembers one doctor, who had a doctorate in analytic chemistry, telling him, "I discovered it was easy to wash walls; the hard part was getting them clean."

Just as important, notes Rabkin, is a lesson in *reversibility*. By exchanging roles, the fledgling physician learned to understand the point of view of other employees in the hospital. "Many doctors were horrified to learn firsthand how often professional people treat nonmedical staff as nonpersons," he says. How well Rabkin understands that reversibility is another cornerstone of attunement.

The Patient's Point of View

Dr. Mitchell Rabkin's regard for each individual and his ability to imagine a patient's point of view were translated into hospital policy, when Beth Israel Hospital became the first hospital in the United States to publish a "patient's bill of rights." This document is believed to have inspired the 1993 law in Massachusetts that guarantees patients access to their own medical records. The bill is a direct result of Rabkin's attunement to the fears of patients who, he believes, are often afraid to ask their busy doctors questions or for a second opinion.

Here is Rabkin's smart summary of the bill's ten points: "You have the right to know what is going on, and when you don't, you can say, 'Hey, wait a minute'—and we won't get sore." The bill's respect for each individual is reflected in its promise that patients have the right to be addressed by their proper name "without undue familiarity." Rabkin explains this phrase by offering a droll description that reveals his ability to reverse roles and imagine the patient's point of view.

"A hospital takes away your name and gives you a number," says Rabkin. "They take away your clothes and give you a 'johnny,' and there seems to be a universal law that at least one of the strings must be missing, so your bare butt is swaying in the breeze. Then, someone comes in saying, 'Wee wee in this pan,' and you say to yourself, 'This morning I was a tiger of industry. What happened?'

So we don't want to add to that; we want to restore the ego of the patient, because then one's strength for inner healing is enhanced."

Even hospital architecture provided Rabkin with an opportunity to express his ability to imagine his patients' and employees' point of view. When Beth Israel was building a new inpatient building, Rabkin collared the architect and insisted that he put a window in the door of the patient's room so the patient could look out into the hospital corridor and the staff could look in.

After the architect, and every other administrator, declared Rabkin crazy, he organized his argument around attunement and told the architect, "Patients want the room to be quiet; yet the only way it can be quiet is to close the door. But why don't doctors and nurses ever close the door? I think it is because they believe that leaving the door open symbolically says 'You have access to me.' So we solve the problem of access *and* quiet by putting a window in the door that looks out onto the corridor. We could symbolize access by having curtains on the door open and create quiet with the door closed."

Rabkin capped his comments by advocating for the individual. "This is a teaching hospital, and professors and students are constantly traipsing in without knocking. With a window on the door, patients could see them coming, have a moment to build their personal defenses, and retain their individuality," he says. Rabkin insisted on the windows and then resisted saying "I told you so" when both staff and patients found them appropriate and useful. The windows are now included in all new patient rooms built at the hospital.

Rabkin's capacity to reverse roles allowed him to look at the architect's plan and to visualize how people might respond to the spaces being created. Three other short examples: He angled the wall so both patients in a double room could see out of the window. He moved the corkboard on which patients post get well cards from the head of the bed, where only doctors and nurses can see it, to the foot of the bed so the patient could see the cards. In addition, he put himself in the nurses' shoes by moving the bathrooms to the back of the new hospital rooms so that nurses, "who stand on their feet all day," wouldn't have to walk extra steps to get by the bathroom every time they entered a room.

Rabkin's ability to understand both patient and employee points of view is also critical to the art of accommodation.

The Whole Story

Mitchell Rabkin was a young physician at the National Institute of Mental Health when he first learned that attunement required *accommodation*—the need to alter an opinion when you hear the whole story. He had been closely following a patient who was admitted to another hospital one weekend and died.

Rabkin remembers, "My first thought was very judgmental: 'Oh, God, they should have known what to do; they should have understood what he needed.' But I called the physician, and it turned out that he had taken every precaution I would have taken and acted on information in the same way that I would have, and the patient died anyway. I thought to myself, 'I'm glad I didn't open my mouth to criticize, but waited to hear the whole story.' "

A second installment of this moment of meaning occurred years later, when Rabkin was CEO of Beth Israel. Here, he learned to seek the whole story in response to positive situations as well as negative ones. He remembers how two employees had quickly carried a person who had been hit by a car in front of the hospital to the emergency room. After Rabkin commended these folks for their lifesaving efforts in his weekly newsletter, another employee came to his office and told Rabkin, "*I* am the one who got the stretcher and took him to the emergency room."

Rabkin calls this episode "Lesson B" and uses it to describe the accommodation attunement requires. "I didn't get the whole story. Whether the news is good or bad, the problem arises when you only get one point of view. Once you voice an opinion, you can't become too emotionally attached to it in the face of the facts. If you are not willing to take on another point of view and change yours, you are in deep yogurt," observes Rabkin.

Anatomy of Attunement

Doctor Rabkin's examples suggest how leaders employ attunement as a habit of mind that organizes their experience with people they lead in several ways. Rabkin conveys his regard for the contribution of each employee by creating non-status name badges and by offering a unique physician's orientation. His reversibility—his capacity to reverse roles and understand another point of view—is evident in his design of hospital rooms and the patient's bill of rights. And he listens for the whole story with colleagues and staff and accommodates his opinion to create a fresh meaning.

Rabkin's anatomy of attunement does not involve the following: deep listening, deep breathing, or lip-synching Aretha Franklin's ode to respect. Instead, attunement is the habit of esteeming the experience and expertise of individuals in an organization. Consider, for example, the senior marketing executive in one of our seminars who shared his Aha! about attunement: "I just realized that it is the people *in the field* who are the experts about these products. I need to start recognizing what they know."

This powerful recognition is also at work in three leaders who celebrate the value of each employee.

Shelly Lazarus, CEO and Chairman, at Ogilvy & Mather: Esteem for Each Employee

Shelly Lazarus refers to herself as "the first female (account manager)" at Ogilvy & Mather. In 1997, on the eve of her twenty-fifth anniversary with the company, she was named its CEO.[2] When asked to describe her rise to the top, Lazarus doesn't review her résumé—for example, her stunning coup of getting IBM to consolidate its $400 million account at Ogilvy & Mather. Instead, she calls O&M a "meritocracy" and adds, "after all this time, the idea of having thirty seconds to get people's attention to sell a product still fascinates me. But for twenty-five years, I have been doing the same job. People just keep showering me with titles!"

Sitting in her Manhattan office, surrounded by her fabled frog collection, Lazarus offers a revealing job description: "My job is to develop talent, to bring people together, and create an atmosphere where they will thrive and do their best work. And I insist that people respect each other's differences and choices."

At a recent meeting of the heads of O&M's European divisions, Lazarus defined the essence of her attunement. In her keynote speech, she summed up her esteem for each individual's contribution by asking her managers, "Can the people who come to work for you come into your office at the end of the day, take their shoes off, and feel comfortable expressing their opinions? Because if they can't, that would concern me. I want everyone in this company to work in an atmosphere where they feel safe, comfortable, and at home." She concluded by reminding her management team, "You have to take care of your people, and I'll take care of you."

The essence of what Lazarus calls "feeling at home" reflects a habit of mind she first observed in her family. As she explains, "My parents helped build my self-confidence by cherishing who I was rather than trying to fashion me in their own image. Whenever I achieved or earned something, they were happy for me, not because of what they wanted me to be. I remember when I was chosen editor of the high school year book; they celebrated it because they knew how important it was to me."

The imprint, or the template, of her parents' influence is apparent in the way she describes her own attunement as a leader, but the style and substance belong to Lazarus. She says, "I start with the belief that people do well in things they are interested in, where they can get excited. I always ask people, 'Where do you want to work? If you could have any job, what would it be?' " And Lazarus practices what she preaches. She once hired a creative director for the Manhattan office who thought he could do his best work by continuing to live on his cattle ranch in Penelope, Texas.

This attunement and regard for each individual in her organization were also underscored in a lesson in leadership by her first boss at Ogilvy & Mather. Twenty-five years ago, when Lazarus was a new account executive and five months pregnant with her first child, her doctor ordered her on complete bed rest. Restless and unable to stay at home for more than one week, she returned to work. On her first day back, then-President Andrew Kershaw called her with an offer she couldn't refuse.

First, Kershaw let her know that he respected her right to make a choice about returning to work. Then he said, "But the least I can do is to be supportive of your choice to return back to work. So I am going to send my personal car to pick you up each day and bring you home until you have your baby."

For Lazarus, Kershaw's kindness and respect created a moment of meaning. "He showed me that nothing is more important to the company than the health, well-being, and strength of the individuals who work here," says Lazarus. She describes how this experience and model from her past are integrated into her present actions as a leader: "Some people need to work three days a week; others need three months to care for a husband who is ill or time for a sabbatical to be refreshed. It is my responsibility to accommodate them. At the end of the day, if I want to continue to be successful in this organization, I have to do what they need as human beings."

Lazarus finds strength in her attunement, even if it means walking out on a client. She once marched her staff out of a meeting with an angry and abusive client by telling him, "You cannot treat my staff this way." As she explains, "I wanted to show my people not to be afraid to stick up for their values." She also recalls that the client was on the phone within minutes, with an apology, and became a loyal and long-standing friend.

The value of each individual was also underlined by another O&M boss, Charles Fredericks, in what Lazarus remembers as the world's shortest performance review. "When I came in, Fredericks said, 'You are doing a great job. Here is $5,000.' " This short lesson spoke volumes to Lazarus, who has translated the message in her own leadership. "We spend so much time on evaluations, when the real purpose is to give people feedback so they can become more successful. There has to be a final accounting of how someone is valued by the organization as a human being," she says. As CEO, Lazarus expresses her regard for each individual by throwing out all of the written forms and encouraging her managers to "write down on paper what the person's true value is."

Each of these examples suggests that Shelly Lazarus has applied the lessons of her experience to craft a habit of mind of attunement, one that allows her to recognize and learn from the expertise of each person in her organization. One former colleague summarized the impact of Lazarus's attunement by noting, "Shelly has the unique knack of making you feel you would do anything for her."

Carolyn McKecuen, Founder and Executive Director, Watermark Association of Artisans: Something to Contribute

Carolyn McKecuen, founder and executive director of Watermark Association of Artisans, received a MacArthur "genius grant" in recognition of her success in building one of the U.S.'s largest craft cooperatives in one of North Carolina's poorest counties.[3] She has been called a cross between Mother Teresa and Donald Trump for training low-income women to make money from the handmade crafts that have been produced in this region since the 1600s. Her statistics sizzle: Watermark sells products from its 740 members to 4,000 companies worldwide, including Ralph Lauren, Esprit, Neiman Marcus, and Walt Disney.

In our conversation with McKecuen, we clearly saw the Trump–Mother Teresa connection. But when we asked her about the legacy of her regard for individuals, we heard echoes of Mae West in her response: "When I was a preteen, I wanted to be a nun, because that is the way I thought I could help people see value within themselves. But then when I became a teenager with hormones, I thought, 'There has to be some other way.' "

When McKecuen took the helm at Watermark, training low-income artisans to market their products, she found a way. Attunement is the essence of her work at Watermark. Here she encourages each artisan's self-regard through economic independence. Her leadership is a fascinating hybrid of her legacy of family and teachers.

McKecuen described her troubled but talented father as a "Jekyll and Hyde personality" who had the gift of attunement. "He was a shoe salesman who could make every customer feel like they were important, the only person in the room," she says. Although he did not bring this gift to his family, McKecuen observed his habit of mind. "I could see what it meant to people and how it could be used to raise children, lead groups, or work with people day to day," she says.

This lesson of regard for each individual was underlined by McKecuen's fifth-grade teacher, a discoverer, who enabled the early blooming, too-tall McKecuen to see the value in herself. McKecuen remembers, "I was ten years old and five-feet-eight. I had no self-assurance; but Mrs. Jamison spent a lot of time with me—showed me I was special. She encouraged me to join organizations like the Girl Scouts, and low and behold, I started winning chairmanships and getting my picture in the papers. She encouraged me to do things I would not have done. That was the first spark anyone had given me."

In her work at Watermark, McKecuen is often the "first spark" in a struggling artisan's life. She recalls a Native American woman she met at a workshop in Northern California: "She had the worst self-esteem I had ever seen. She held her head down, never asked a question."

When McKecuen learned this woman had been trying to learn to carve sandstone, she asked her to bring her pieces in. "The figures were quite gorgeous—a small angel and a dinosaur. When I asked if I could buy them, she began to cry. She realized that she had made something of enough worth for someone to buy it," says McKecuen.

She also underlines her regard for Watermark staff members by recognizing their authority. As McKecuen explains, "No matter where you are in the chain of command, everyone has something to contribute. But sometimes, you have to ask for it." She offers the example of asking Katerina, a warehouse worker, for suggestions. Katerina asked McKecuen, "You really want me to tell you how it could work better?" McKecuen reassured her, "Katerina, I don't work in that shipping department, you do. If you have some ideas, we should talk about it." As a result, McKecuen began receiving several useful suggestions each week.

McKecuen's attunement is enhanced by her capacity for accommodation. With her signature good humor, she offers a moment of meaning about hearing the whole story. Her story revolves around calling each of the three women who had worked on a quilt to give them the news that actor Paul Newman had bought the quilt at a shop in Westport, Connecticut.

As McKecuen tells it: "I called the first woman and told her, 'Paul Newman just bought your quilt.' She said, 'If he likes it, just give it to him.' I called the second woman, and she said, 'My husband and kids said that I would never sell anything. I'm not going to give them any of this money.' I called the third woman, who was eighty years old, and said, 'Paul Newman just bought your quilt.' She was silent, and I thought maybe she didn't know who he was. So I started to explain, and she said, 'Oh, I know who he is. I was just picturing Paul Newman's buns on *my* quilt.' "

McKecuen chuckled at the memory of telling this politically incorrect story when she accepted the Ms. Foundation's first Economic Justice Award at Manhattan's tourist-filled but festive Rainbow Room. But she is serious about the importance of learning the whole story and the willingness to change your point of view. She says, "It reminded me of how one life experience—whether getting a check or making a sale—doesn't mean the same thing to each person."

This lesson allows her to be attuned to her impact as a leader. Whether she is talking to corporate sponsors or technical assistants, McKecuen makes sure that everyone is following her train of thought. "When I make a statement, three different people will get three different takes," she says. "You can't just throw out an idea and assume that everybody understands it. So I have to say to myself, 'Am I explaining this correctly? Is everybody getting this? Is someone not understanding, but too shy to speak up?' "

Ellen Bravo is another leader whose regard for each individual's contribution is the essence of her attunement.

Ellen Bravo, Codirector, 9 to 5: Letting Brilliant Thoughts Flourish

As codirector of 9 to 5, the National Association of Working Women, Ellen Bravo is a leading spokesperson about pay equity, family leave, and sexual harassment. Her appearances on television and at public forums have been described as moving, witty, and sometimes bawdy. Yet Bravo's leadership is defined by listening. As she puts it, "Sometimes the best leadership is being quiet, getting out of the way of other people. I like debating, I like inspiring people, but doing this job involves taking lessons on how to listen—to allow others to recognize their own leadership."

Bravo's attunement is driven by respect for each person's leadership potential. For Bravo, attunement is a model for a collaborative style of leadership, one inspired by her participation in the women's movement and guided by her purpose of building a diverse, no top-dogs organization at 9 to 5. She talks about a moment of meaning that taught her "what some people call leadership is, in fact, the silencing of other people."

Bravo had called a meeting to address the fact that although 9 to 5 called itself a multiracial organization all of the leadership was white. Bravo's solution—to create a leadership team where one-third of the women would be of color—was met by less than a standing ovation. When Bravo explored the tepid reception, she discovered a whole layer of meaning that wasn't being challenged. The staff and members wanted more substantial change; they wanted to look at the ways that decisions were made in the organization. As a result, Bravo called an outside consultant to explore how to transform the organization in a more fundamental way.

The lesson for Bravo was clear: "I used to think that being a leader meant taking the initiative, being the one to make the proposal that other people respond to. Now I think of my role as a leader in terms of creating the situation in which many people can make proposals. I don't want to lead an endless meeting where everyone discusses each point. I want to maximize the opportunities for everyone's brilliant thoughts to flourish."

To create this opportunity for brilliant thoughts, Bravo became attuned to different learning styles. As she elaborated, "I'm very verbal, so my style works best with people who have an auditory learning style. But not everyone learns by hearing. Some need to see it, or feel it, and shape it in a different way." Bravo also examined her own speed-of-light mode of thinking and talking. She jokes, "Someone once told me that I think too fast. And since there is not much I can do about that, I have encouraged and learned to live with a decision style where people can take time for reflection and use their own ways of processing information."

Bravo's regard for individuals in her organization defines her leadership and shapes her actions. For her, attunement means giving power to more and more people. In this model, a leader succeeds only when people connect with their own power to lead. Her portrait of a person's discovery of her own leadership is deeply moving.

As Bravo explains, "You see the moment when it switches from women thinking that someone else can make this happen to the moment when they see themselves as part of it. And they understand the why and the how. You can see the effect this has on their sense of themselves and their lives. When they make progress— even if they don't change the law or get their job back—they see a victory; nothing will be the same as it was. They know that the person who treated them badly will have a harder time doing it to somebody else."

Constructing Attunement

Bravo, McKecuen, Lazarus, and Rabkin each described events of knowing they have translated into a commitment to regard and learn from the individuals in their organization. Bravo's convincing insight came from reading the silence that greeted her suggestion of a leadership team. Lazarus learned from exemplars who esteemed her choices and contributions. McKecuen leveraged the lesson of Paul Newman's quilt purchase. And Rabkin applied the attunement from the psychiatrist who recognized each person's rich qualities.

Each leader's insight then became a personal *construct*—a way of interpreting, or "construing," the behavior of people around him. According to psychologist George Kelley, constructs are the categories that people use to code information about themselves and the abilities and intentions of others.[4]

To understand constructs in action, consider George Kelley's moment of meaning. Kelley developed his theory of personal constructs on the road as a traveling psychologist who visited schools throughout Kansas. He observed that teachers who labeled, or construed, various children as "lazy" tended to have plenty of other problems in their classrooms. In his attempt to change the label, or construct, a teacher used, Kelley encouraged the teachers to insist that "lazy children do nothing."

Teachers discovered that what the so-called lazy children did, after being encouraged to be lazy, offered them a different understanding of these kids. In fact, many of the laziest students came up with the most inventive ideas. And teachers found that the construct "laziness" had been used in situations where the students didn't understand or enjoy the lesson. When the teachers changed their construct about these children and saw them as inventive or alternately as bored, they were able to expect and get more participation from them.

Teachers, like leaders, behave according to their own constructs; so when they anticipate and expect lazy behavior, they get it. In contrast, when a leader and teacher like Rabkin, Bravo, or McKecuen operates out of the construct of the "richness" in each individual, the anticipation of getting the best from each person can shape his or her behavior.

With his construct of regard, Rabkin's attunement allows him to see beyond the doctors' dining room, the name badges, and hospital gowns and bracelets to consider each person of equal worth. Similarly, Bravo sees the leadership potential of each staff member, and McKecuen encourages artisans to see the value of their work.

A conversation with Chicago Cubs president Andy MacPhail highlighted another element of attunement. Looking back on his first year as the thirty-three-year-old general manager of the Minnesota Twins, MacPhail described how his ability to reverse roles was critical to his selection of the field manager who took the Twins to the pennant.

Andy MacPhail, President, Chicago Cubs: Making the Team

Baseball's Hall of Fame reads like a family album for Andy MacPhail. His grandfather, Larry MacPhail, was owner of the legendary Brooklyn Dodgers and the New York Yankees; and his father, Lee MacPhail, served as general manager of the Baltimore Orioles and the New York Yankees and as president of the American League.

According to MacPhail, his father's fair-mindedness—his ability to imagine another viewpoint—created a model for attunement. This habit of mind ripened in MacPhail's leadership as the thirty-year-old manager of the World Series–winning Minnesota Twins. Decades later, his attunement supported Chicago Cubs's slugger Sammy Sosa in the home-run sweepstakes with Mark McGwire.

MacPhail explains, "You could discuss about any topic with my father from baseball to current events. When I expressed indignation and asked, 'How could he *do* that?' my father would describe how the person could. If I was griping about an agent, my father would remind me of the pressure an agent feels to make good deals. He told me not to get so caught up in my point of view that I forget to see what is important to the other guy."

MacPhail translated the legacy of his father's attunement when he became general manager of the Minnesota Twins. As he looks back to that first winning season, he understands how his belief in his own judgment was strengthened by his ability to reverse roles and to stand in owner Carl Pohlad's shoes.

When MacPhail was hired, he wanted to bring along thirty-seven-year-old Tom Kelly as his field manager. Having watched Kelly manage a number of games and talk to the players, MacPhail was convinced that Kelly was right for the Twins. Yet he was having a difficult time convincing Pohlad to give him final approval. MacPhail remembers, "It took me a long time to figure out what Carl's concerns were. I knew he liked Tom. But once I understood his point of view, I could reconfigure the situation and solve his problem and mine."

When he reversed roles, MacPhail understood that Pohlad had made a sizable investment in the Twins and the two boy wonders made him a bit edgy. He was reluctant to turn the team over to the youngest tandem to ever take these jobs. "After all," says MacPhail, "he's in the business of building the public's perception, and the public will always demand to know a reason to believe in the team. Tom and I were so young; we had no box office appeal."

Once MacPhail understood Pohlad's view, he hired Kelly, along with former Yankees general manager Ralph Houk. With the more-seasoned Houk aboard, Pohlad got the element of experience he needed. Strengthened by MacPhail's capacity for attunement, his management team brought the Twins to the pennant that year.

Years later, as the Chicago Cubs's president, MacPhail's attunement has been key in his relationship with superstar Sammy Sosa. For him, Sosa's success is especially sweet. MacPhail says, "When we signed him, the contract was lucrative, controversial, and much criticized—many people said it was too much money. But when you spend a quiet five minutes with him, you understand that he has the character to justify the investment. He takes pride in his accomplishment, and responsibility for his actions. He wants to give something back to the game."

During the summer of Sosa's slugfest with Mark McGwire, MacPhail put himself in Sosa's shoes and kept his distance. As he explains, "Sammy had his hands full with every game. He had so much on his plate that he didn't need my input as another level of distraction. The greater the scrutiny of the media, the further I tried to back away."

Sosa expressed his appreciation of MacPhail's attunement the night the Cubs won the 1998 playoffs and partied before traveling to a postseason game in Atlanta. On the evening of the victory celebration, MacPhail's secretary called him to deliver Sosa's message: "Tell Andy Sammy won't go to Atlanta tomorrow unless he comes to the party tonight."

Attunement as Reversibility

Andy MacPhail's role reversal and Mitchell Rabkin's ability to picture the patient in bed and the doctors in the hallway illustrate how attunement enables leaders to understand what Robert Kegan calls "a reality quite different from my own."[5] This reversibility, says Kegan, is the ability of one person to take on the role of another person. In this role reversal, we see the other's behavior is the consequence of a stimulus that is quite distinct from our own point of view.

To understand reversibility, consider the wonderful homework assignment of one of our daughters. Hannah was asked to rewrite several classic fairy tales from the villain's point of view. In these fractured fairy tales, her teacher encouraged her to wonder, What was the child-napping, grandma-gulping wolf's point of view? What was the witch's gripe when Rapunzel's father trashes her garden by pulling up all the rampion weed?

Andy MacPhail did his own version of this homework when he asked himself, How does Carl Pohlad see my choice of field manager? And Rabkin's reversibility led him to ask how patients feel when they lie in a hospital bed and how doctors feel when they enter the room to care for a patient or work on the housekeeping staff.

We have introduced a number of leaders whose attunement was marked by this capacity for reversibility. For example, Patricia Gallup, PC Connection's CEO, traces her attunement to customers to her childhood dinners when she and her sisters practiced reversibility by role playing various points of view in the labor disputes their father mediated.

Now consider Gun Denhart, president and founder of Hanna Andersson, the premier children's clothing catalog. Her attunement and role-taking ability led to a defining moment for the company's widely praised policy of subsidizing 50 percent of its employees' child care costs. As Denhart tells the story, "I remember talking to a woman with her two small children in my office. I looked at her paycheck and I looked at the children, and I thought, 'How does this work?' " Denhart's attunement shaped the beginning of a company policy to subsidize working parents.

Finally, we note how banking executive Anat Bird moved from New York to St. Louis and packed her unique style of attunement as accommodation.

Anat Bird, COO, Roosevelt Bank: Tell Her the Truth

When Israeli-born, New York–based financial consultant Anat Bird was named chief operating officer of Roosevelt Bank in Missouri, employees expected the worst. Said one, "I wasn't sure I wanted to work for an Israeli tank commander." Another employee wondered, "What could someone from New York bring to St. Louis?"

Here's what they didn't know about Anat Bird. Her father, an Israeli steel trader, had showed her how to treat all people with respect—from the dockworkers at his plant to Prime Minister Menachem Begin. And her military experience had taught her the importance of teams. This legacy was translated in her transition strategy: she planned to visit each of Roosevelt's 1,300 employees during her first six weeks on the job.

Anat Bird describes how the resource of attunement was critical to her transition into the Midwestern banking community: "When I arrived, I told them, 'I'm not a New Yorker who's going to bring my crew and wreck the joint. I'm going to integrate myself into the company and not the other way around.' " And then, Bird listened. She went to every single branch and talked to every employee. She asked, "Forget about the $9 billion. If this was your bank, what would you do?"

For Bird, a consultant who had spent years "being paid to tell people what to do," her new role as leader posed a unique challenge. As she recalls, "I wasn't sure that I could touch so many people at the same time, to unify and inspire them to work toward a single goal. In all of my consulting work, the 'Aha!' was my Aha; the conclusion was mine. This time, I just collected information; I didn't proccss; I listened and kept my mouth shut." Bird's transition to leadership succeeded because of her ability to use attunement as a way of accommodating, or of hearing the whole story and making a fresh meaning after taking her employees' views into account.

Shortly after Bird came to St. Louis a CNN reporter interviewed several employees about their reaction to Bird's leadership. One branch manager admitted to being intimidated by stories about Bird's success and smarts. When he visited her branch, he had decided just to answer her questions and listen. But instead, he says, "In about fifteen minutes, I found myself opening up and telling her everything I knew about Roosevelt and what I wanted to do here. She listened and told me, 'Let's do it together.' " Another manager opined, "She really gets where we are coming from at the branches. She understands what obstacles we face, and she'll do whatever she can to make it work for us."

Bird believes that her evolution from listening to the conversation in her own mind to listening to the employees' point of view would only succeed if employees told her the truth. "So many executives don't have a clue," says Bird. "They operate on anecdotal information: A spouse or board member goes into a branch, and they build a whole story around it. I didn't want to make that mistake, so I told employees from the beginning not to tell me what they think I wanted to hear."

Anat Bird's attunement—her capacity to accommodate knowledge and ideas from her employees—is a key to her leadership. One manager summed up Bird's attunement by saying, "She's interested in what you have to say, so tell her the truth, because she wants to help you. And that's how problems get solved."

Attunement as Accommodation

Anat Bird sought the whole story by visiting every branch in the bank. For Mitchell Rabkin, getting the whole story—whether it is about a patient who died or the ER staffer who saved a life—means that he might have to change his opinion in the face of someone else's perspective. Both leaders have avoided the trap of becoming too attached to their own point of view. This tension is detailed by Swiss psychologist Jean Piaget, who would frame attunement as a struggle between *assimilation*—fitting new experiences into our old schemes of meaning—and *accommodation,* or recognizing our old ways of making meaning to take new experiences into account.[6]

Rabkin's and Bird's accommodation—their willingness to embrace a new meaning based on other points of view—reminded us of a much-repeated story of a smart upstart who goes to visit the village wise woman. Instead of listening, he talks. To interrupt his monologue, the wise one offers him a cup of tea. As he holds out his cup, she continues to pour until the tea splashes on the ground. "Our interview is over," says the wise woman, "Because when you came here, your cup was already full."

Attunement is the habit of mind that leaves room in a leader's cup.

A Fresh Perspective

The leaders we have described have demonstrated the richness of attunement as a habit of mind, one that organizes the way they think about the people they lead. Consider Anat Bird tuning into the branch banks, Carolyn McKecuen encouraging artisans, Andy MacPhail standing in Sammy Sosa's shoes, or Ellen Bravo listening to the silence, and you can view the essence of attunement as a resource that is both generous and generative.

The attunement of these leaders echoes philosopher Edmund Husserl's suggestion that we can freshen our perspective by "bracketing," or setting aside our assumptions about the world.[7] Then when we experience new things, we can get past the layers of meaning we have built up. In the act of attunement, leaders put their assumptions on hold and begin to recognize and learn from the authority of each person they encounter.

Mitchell Rabkin illustrates the act of bracketing with a story about sitting down to lunch with a custodian whom he recognized only as the person who cleaned the corridors outside his office. In their conversation, Rabkin discovered that for seventeen years, this employee had worked from 7:00 A.M. to 3:00 P.M. at Beth Israel Hospital and from 3:00 P.M. to 11:00 P.M. in another hospital. The double shift had allowed him to send each of his nine children to graduate school. His oldest child was a professor of microbiology at Stanford; another child was a law professor at Yale.

Rabkin recalls, "I had been walking past this man and all I saw was someone pushing a broom. I had no idea of the human being within. It is important to assume richness lies there, to treat everyone as if they have these qualities, and to convey the sense that we are all colleagues." Here, Rabkin defines the agenda of attunement.

NOTEBOOK: ATTUNEMENT

Care Group CEO Dr. Mitchell Rabkin talked about being inspired by the psychiatrist who treated patients, family, and staff with equal respect.

- Think of a parent, teacher, boss, or colleague who showed you a similar example of attunement as regard to each individual or who demonstrated a lack of regard. How have you (or could you) apply the lesson of these examples in your leadership?

- How do you demonstrate the importance and contribution of each individual in your organization?

For 9 to 5 codirector Ellen Bravo, attunement is a means of avoiding "leadership by silencing" and allowing "brilliant thoughts to flourish."

- Recall people or experiences in your life that have offered you a similar model of leadership by listening instead of talking. What were the key behaviors you observed?

- How do you (or can you) encourage the leadership and "brilliant thoughts" of the people who work in your organization?

By drawing upon his father's fair-mindedness, Chicago Cubs president Andy MacPhail honed his ability to reverse roles. This reversibility was critical in understanding Minnesota Twins owner Carl Pohlad's objections to MacPhail's hiring decisions and creating a winning team.

- Identify a parent, teacher, friend, boss, or colleague whose behavior was a model of reversing roles to understand another point of view. How have you translated this example in your leadership?

- Describe a time when your willingness to reverse roles to understand the viewpoint of someone in your organization was the key to resolving a problem. Or recall a time when your lack of attunement created a roadblock in resolving an issue. Summarize your insights about these experiences.

Roosevelt Bank COO Anat Bird's capacity to seek and accommodate knowledge and ideas from her employees was a key to her transition to leadership.

(continued)

- List the leaders and experiences in your life that have provided models of setting aside assumptions to accommodate a fresh perspective. How have you (or might you) translated these examples into your leadership?

- Consider a time when you changed your opinion after you learned someone else's sense of the story. Or recall a situation when you stuck to your story, created understanding, or prolonged the problem. How have you incorporated these lessons about attunement in the way you lead your organization?

Chapter 7

Conviction

Relying on Inner Authority

M ore than thirty years ago, Fred Rogers, CEO of Family Communications and executive producer of *Mister Rogers' Neighborhood*, went to New York for an interview to replace the host of a children's program.[1] The first thing the producer asked him is what he would wear. Rogers answered that he would always wear his own clothes. When the producer insisted that he would have to wear a costume to "get the kids," Rogers said, "I think this is probably the end of the meeting."

In the three decades since Fred Rogers conveyed this unique conviction about the kind of clothes that make the man, his jello-colored cardigans—knitted by his mother—have been satirized by Eddie Murphy on *Saturday Night Live*, displayed at the Smithsonian Museum and featured on the cover of *Esquire*. *Mister Rogers' Neighborhood*, where Rogers celebrates "what's inside" of each child and often sings, "It's you I like, it's not the things you wear," has become the longest-running show in public television history.

"I've been truly blessed that the people at PBS would support my hunches," Rogers says. "There will always be something new coming along that will take people's attention for a while, but there is always that which is real. And I think that the greatest gift you can give anybody is the gift of your honest self. Anytime I have ever seen compelling television—take Julia Child, for example—it has been people who have *dared to be themselves*."

In a single phrase—"daring to be themselves"—Rogers captures the conviction that anchors his leadership of two organizations: Family Communications, the nonprofit organization he founded to produce educational materials for teachers, children, and families; and *Mister Rogers' Neighborhood*, the program that has allowed Fred Rogers to become a trusted "television neighbor" to three generations of families. When we explore how Fred Rogers dares to be himself, we glimpse several elements of *conviction* that anchor and focus leaders: purpose, self-consistency, and inner authority. Leaders like Fred Rogers describe conviction as a habit of mind defined by trusting, valuing, and speaking from one's own experience.[2]

Consider, first, how Fred Rogers pursued his purpose by linking the legacy of his past and present experiences.

A Purpose for Television

"I had every childhood disease that came down the pike," says Rogers, recalling his childhood in the small industrial town of Latrobe, Pennsylvania.[3] It was a town he describes as "one big neighborhood," where his father's McFeely Brick Company was one of the largest employers. His attentive, protective mother discouraged him from playing outdoors alone and once tried to cure his hay fever by keeping him in an air-conditioned room during ragweed season.

Rogers filled this solitary time with the kind of puppet play and music that now delight the pint-size audience of *Mister Rogers' Neighborhood*. Yet it was a moment of meaning on his grandfather's farm that suggested the sense of purpose Rogers brings to work every day.

Grandpa McFeely was determined to declare his grandson's independence, even allowing eight-year-old Fred to walk along the stone wall his parents had deemed too dangerous. Then one day, at the end of a visit, his grandfather spoke the words that would later be transformed into Mister Rogers's signature celebration of each child. "You made this day special just by being yourself," said Grandpa. "Remember there is just one person in this world like you, and I like you just the way you are."

Yet it would be many years before Rogers leveraged this lesson into his unique approach to children's programming. In fact, he didn't even see a television until he came home for Easter vacation his senior year at Rollins College in Florida. He was a music composition major with plans to enter the Presbyterian seminary in the fall when he switched on his parents' new television for the first time.

It was hate at first sight. "I loved radio as a kid; but I saw this new medium in my parents' home being used to show people demeaning each other—with putdowns and pies in faces. I just felt there was something that could be done with this medium that would be healthier than that," he says.

After graduating from college, Rogers moved to New York and worked on *The Voice of Firestone*, *Lucky Strike Hit Parade*, and *The Gabby Hayes Show*. He moved to Pittsburgh several years later at the request of WQED, the nation's first community-supported public television station. There he helped develop *The Children's Corner*, creating many of the puppet characters that would later appear on *Mister Rogers' Neighborhood*. During his seven years of working on the show, he studied child development and attended Pittsburgh Theological Seminary during his lunch hours.

Following his seminary school graduation and while he was preparing to enter the ministry, Rogers received an offer from the Canadian Broadcasting Company to go to Toronto and create a show called *MISTERROGERS*. Two years later, he renamed the show and brought it back to Pittsburgh. Through this new show, public television became his pulpit. His congregation includes more than 3 million U.S. households each week.

To watch Fred Rogers, whether on television or speaking at a college graduation, is to understand how he has transformed two events of knowing—the love and freedom he experienced on his grandfather's farm and his troubling first encounter with television—into a powerful and consistent purpose. His devotion to daring young people (and their parents) to be themselves, to love without conditions, and to join the adventure of play resonates in his every word and deed.

For example: He signs off every show with a version of his grandfather's encouraging words. To his guest confined to a wheelchair, he sings his anthem of unconditional regard: "It's you I like, the way you are right now. The things inside you, not the things that hide you." He even offered the youthful graduates at Boston University a similar message by quoting from Antoine de Saint-Exupéry's *The Little Prince*: "What is essential is invisible to the eye." Then he asked them, "What is essential about you that is invisible to the eye?"

Walking Stories

How does Fred Rogers's conviction about being genuine connect with his vast electronic congregation? As he explains, "We human beings are walking stories and we long to be connected with other stories. We want to test our stories in relationship with other people's stories. So the more real we can be, the more we can communicate the eternal verities of this life that we all long to be in touch with."

Rogers's understanding of the way stories connect was the unexpected lesson from listening to a minister deliver "the worst sermon I have ever heard in my life." On a long-ago summer visit to a chapel on Nantucket Island, Rogers turned to his friend, Dottie Barbour, to complain about the sermon and was shocked to see that she had tears running down her cheeks. She whispered, "He said exactly what I needed to hear." For Rogers, this moment of meaning yielded a compelling insight. "I had come in judgment, and she had come in need," he says. "I became convinced that the space between the person who is speaking and the person in need is a holy ground and can be used that way."

This insight has shaped his point of view about broadcasting. Rogers says, "I feel the same way about the television—that we do the best we can, give the best that we know how, and the Spirit takes it from the screen to whoever comes in need. Through the years, we've had amazing reports about what has been transferred to people's hearts. There are so many instances in which this medium can be abused, but it can also be gracefully used.".

He remembers the letter from a mother who was not allowed

in the room for her daughter's cancer radiation treatments. When her daughter wanted to know how long the treatment would take and she couldn't understand how long a minute was, her mother started singing Mister Rogers's opening song "It's a Beautiful Day in the Neighborhood." "That's what a minute is," the mother said. Her daughter replied, "Oh, I can take it for that long. Will you sing it while I'm doing it?"

Then, Rogers explains, "they rigged up a loudspeaker in the treatment room so that every time that child had radiation, her mother sang 'It's a Beautiful Day in the Neighborhood.' And that was their minute." Of his role in connecting with the child in this "walking story," he said, "It's wonderful to think that I could be of help in situations that are potentially frightening for children. I love when families use our work in that way. It's a great blessing."

Consider, finally, how Fred Rogers practices what he preaches. His Emmy acceptance speech included a brave request that broadcast his lifelong purpose and self-consistency. Witness how his inner authority led the evening in an unexpectedly graceful direction.

Daring to Be Himself

When Fred Rogers walked to the podium to accept television's highest honor—an Emmy Lifetime Achievement Award—he bowed and then stunned the tanned and bejeweled audience by requesting silence. He began, "All of us have special ones who have loved us into being. Would you just take, along with me, ten seconds to think of the people who have allowed you to become who you are. . . . Ten seconds of silence." He looked at his watch and announced, "I'll watch the time."

One media maven described the scene as follows: "There was at first, a giddy, strangled hiccup of laughter as people realized that he wasn't kidding. . . . One second, two seconds, three seconds, and now the jaws clenched, the bosoms heaved, the mascara ran, and the tears fell on the gathering like rain leaking from a crystal chandelier."[4]

Fred Rogers's description is less florid: "When I walked in, I thought, 'Do I dare to do this?' I mean, it was so loud. It was like a circus. But I wanted to give some quiet time in the midst of all this bustle, to allow people to go as deep within themselves as they wanted. When I looked out, I saw thoughtful faces, people who had tears in their eyes. The whole tenor of the place seemed different."

We wondered, Was this the holy ground between the speaker and the person in need? "I guess that did happen," says Fred Rogers. "It was a wonderful confirmation of knowing that what's really important is what's inside."

The Crux of Conviction

Fred Rogers suggests that conviction is a distinct kind of authority that results from a leader's awareness and transformation of their life experiences. Psychologist Elizabeth Debold expands this definition by pointing out that the words *authority* and *author* have the same root—an ancient French word that means "to grow, originate, to promote or increase."[5]

Rogers originated—became author of—his sense of purpose by translating his grandfather's message of self-acceptance into a no-pies-in-the-face children's program. In daring children to be themselves, he models and promotes self-consistency. In his Emmy acceptance speech, he relied on his inner authority to increase the audience's focus on "what's inside."

Among all the habits of mind we have studied, the link between a leader's legacy and his or her conviction stands out. Yet it is a leader's legacy that distinguishes conviction from the familiar business buzzwords of *values* and *vision*. Conviction is a habit of mind that enables leaders to translate their legacy by creating a precise meaning for the goals and standards of their leadership. In this way, conviction anchors a leader's authority in a wisdom won by experience.

We can underscore this authority by studying the leadership of a remarkable scientist, Dr. Leroy Hood.

Dr. Leroy Hood, Gates Chair and Chairman, Department of Molecular Biotechnology, University of Washington: The Scientist as Educator

Biotechnologist Dr. Leroy Hood is one of the founding fathers of the Human Genome Project and the inventor of such brave new machines as the DNA fluorescence sequencer, which allows researchers to catalog in one day the genetic data that once took a year to encode. He is widely recognized as a leader who will shepherd genetic science into an astonishing new age. His prophecies about biotechnology can be both dazzling and unsettling. Consider, for example, his prediction that by 2020 all Americans will carry credit card–size plastic strips that contain computer readouts of their personal genomes.[6]

For those who didn't watch *Bill Nye, the Science Guy*, a genome consists of the 100,000 genes encoded by 3 billion chemical pairs in our DNA. Hood's purpose in mapping human genomes is compelling and clear: It's about preventive medicine that can alleviate human suffering. "We'll be able to do a DNA fingerprint on each individual," suggests Hood. "The computer will read out your future health history, and we will have preventative measures that allow us to intervene and cure many of the diseases that plague mankind."

Hood's purpose and predictions prompted Microsoft mogul Bill Gates to dub the genome "the most advanced program around" and to offer the University of Washington $12 million, no strings attached, to persuade Hood to leave his position at the California Institute of Technology in Pasadena and to start a Department of Molecular Biotechnology. Recently, the former junk bond dealer, Michael Milken, who suffers from prostate cancer, pledged $20 million to create a cure-seeking consortium headed by Hood.

Still, amid all the clamor for Hood's leadership, the most fascinating facet of his inner work was this conviction that the scientist's purpose is not just to be a discoverer and inventor, but to be an educator. "Making machines is an important part of what I do, but it is subservient to the idea of being an integrator and a synthesizer.

I feel I have an enormous obligation to communicate science to the public in a really effective way," he says.

Mapping the source of Hood's passion about educating the distrustful, often hostile public about hot-button genetic research, we found that all roads lead to Montana. He was raised in Missoula and Shelby, where his mother gave him enormous freedom—allowing her seven-year-old son to camp and hike alone in the mountains. For Hood, the legacy of this lack of constraint was "the sense that you could determine your own path."

As one of the 140 students at Shelby High School, Hood thrived on his big-frog-in-a-small-pond status. He remembers, "At Shelby High School, like other rural environments, there were no limits. So I was quarterback of the football team, I participated in the theater and on the debate team, I worked on the newspaper and the annual. I think if I had gone to a bigger school, I would have had a different picture of myself. My high school experience left me with the unbreakable feeling that I could do anything, that I could set my own agenda and not be dictated to by the agenda of other people."

Clearly, his mother's support of the solo hikes and Hood's extracurricular successes nourished an inner authority that has allowed him to persist in his purpose of mapping genomes as preventive medicine. But there is one more critical piece of Hood's legacy as a purposeful leader: how becoming a student teacher planted the second purpose of becoming a scientist-cum-educator.

Hood recalls an event of knowing when in his senior year his chemistry teacher, Clifford Olson, tapped him to teach biology to freshmen and sophomore students. "I would read these articles in *Scientific American* and try to get the students excited about the ideas. It was a marvelous experience. Because you can't use jargon. You have to talk about what the ideas are all about. The experience taught me the importance of being able to articulate issues and get people excited about them," he says.

Hood's ability to educate his peers and rely on his inner authority became a key to his success, particularly during the bad old days when much of the scientific community refused to embrace the teachers or inventors of the new science, biotechnology. For example, when Cal Tech professor Hood approached his department in the early 1980s to join him in marketing the first prototype of a high-speed DNA protein sequencer he had developed, his colleagues refused to mix business and research. Hood then approached nineteen private firms, but they also turned him down. Fueled by his inner authority, he created his own firm, Biosystems, Inc., to develop a machine that Nobel laureate James Watson later called "the workhorse of the Human Genome Project."

Hood also received a remarkably rude reception as a summer guest speaker about the Human Genome Project at the Woods Hole Conference Center on Cape Cod. He recalls, "When the lecture ended—and after I endured all of the hostile, aggressive, and defensive questions—even the *host* who had invited me to give the lecture disappeared. I had to walk back to my motel alone."

Hood endured this pommeling by focusing on his purpose. "I felt beat up, but I never felt that I was wrong. Sometimes you have to separate the benefits of science from the people who do it. For every difficulty, every challenging ethical issue, it is important to keep in mind that the real purpose is to alleviate human suffering," he says.

When Bill Gates approached Hood to create a chair and Department of Molecular Biotechnology at the University of Washington, Hood was able to shift his priority from educating his peers to educating the public. "At the start of the department, I said, 'We are about two things: systems biology and communicating to the public.' That was my opening gambit," says Hood.

In the Biotechnology Department that Leroy Hood has built, communicating with the public is part of the job description. Here, even the students in the doctorate programs are required to give a fifteen-minute speech on their dissertation to a lay audience. In this purpose, Hood leads by example from coauthoring a book on bioethics, *The Code of Codes*, to accepting dozens of media and speaking engagements in such wide-ranging venues as church suppers, class reunions, the Elks Club, and the halls of Congress. When television's Barbara Walters wondered about manipulating genes to create a perfect baby, it was Hood who explained the practical impossibility.

And when Hood asks to see the manager of a restaurant, it is not because there is a fly in his soup. Instead, he wants to discuss the poster that proclaims "We serve no genetically altered foods." Does Hood change the manager's mind? "Almost never," concedes Hood, who adds, "I'm very pessimistic about changing adult attitudes in a short-term interaction. But I'm very optimistic about being able to train kids to develop inquiry-based thinking, to be open to these ideas."

Hood offered the example of a lesson from a comprehensive kindergarten through twelfth-grade (K-12) curriculum developed by his department. In a high school class that was learning how to do DNA sequencing, they divided students into groups of four and asked them to pretend they were a family that had the trait for Huntington's disease. Then the students were given instructions about how to think analytically about the associated ethical problems. They also received hypothetical diagnoses so they could talk about their implications in the context of the family. "At the end of that time, the kids understood a lot about the dilemmas posed by human genetics," says Hood.

Teaching in this K-12 program is one of the ways a faculty member fulfills Hood's expectation that they spend 5 to 10 percent of their time in outreach activities, including parent and community education or lobbying school boards for more science funds. "My department chair colleagues at other universities tell me that they are too busy for this kind of outreach," says Hood, "but the best way we can communicate with the public is through kids. I can think of nothing more important than educating our kids. I would put that at the top of any list I make."

The Practice of Purpose

Each leader's purpose is informed by an approach to conviction that reaches back to antiquity. The ancient Greeks used the word *teleology* to refer to the evaluation of conduct in relation to ends, goals, and purposes.[7] This approach to conduct is a key in understanding Fred

Rogers's commitment to daring children to be themselves and Leroy Hood's passion about educating the public. It is also striking to note that both Hood's and Rogers's purpose as leaders are anchored by self-consistency and inner authority.

These elements of conviction are apparent in leaders described in earlier chapters as well. Remember Ogilvy & Mather CEO Shelly Lazarus's goal of building an atmosphere where talented people could do their best work; Beckie Masaki's purpose of strengthening the Asian American community by creating a sanctuary for battered women, and Esther Torres's keeping her eye on "the end of the matter" by rechanneling the energy of homeless youth in her community development program.

Each of these leaders acted out of unique and consistent convictions born of their legacy. Like Hood and Rogers, each of them evaluated her own conduct as a leader in terms of her purpose. Each was anchored by an inner authority. We also saw how Bill Shore, executive director of Share Our Strength, keeps fighting hunger by relying on a guiding metaphor, one shaped by viewing the great cathedrals of Europe.

Shore's metaphor reminds us of a much-told tale about how purpose is practiced. Three stone masons toil to build the ancient Cathedral of Notre Dame in Paris. When asked about his job, one mason sighs and says, "I carry heavy stones around all day." A second mason explains, "I'm building a wall." But the third speaks with the end purpose in mind: "I'm building a cathedral," he proudly reports.

If you prefer a more modern perspective about a leader's mindful purpose, just remember that baseball's leading funny bone, Yogi Berra, was wrong when he insisted that you can't think and hit the ball at the same time.

Two compelling leaders further illuminate conviction as a habit of mind: Ed Lewis, chairman and CEO of Essence Communications, whose self-consistency has created a powerful inner authority; and Dave Duffield, president and CEO of PeopleSoft, who relies on his inner authority to share a corporate culture with a consistent and unique purpose.

Ed Lewis, Chairman and CEO, Essence Communications: Consistent Conviction

It has been more than thirty years since Ed Lewis left Citibank's executive training program to become the cofounder of *Essence Magazine*, the first magazine to chronicle the lives and careers of African American women. Lewis launched *Essence* with $130,000, a press run of 50,000, and thirteen advertising pages and presided over its growth into a $100 million publishing business with 1,000 ad pages per year and a readership of nearly 8 million.[8]

In *Essence*—and a new magazine, *Latino Women*—his readers hear the vibrant voice of women of color and the echo of Lewis's family legacy of powerful women. Lewis was raised in the South Bronx in New York City, where his father worked for twenty-five years at minimum wage as a janitor at City College. But it was his mother—a beautician, school crossing guard, and factory worker— who nurtured his convictions. "Be a good man, be a proud black man, and do the right thing," she told Lewis.

Lewis found his mother, grandmother, and cousin, Susannah models of consistent conviction. Through their words and deeds, they taught him to take a stand on tough issues. On a summer bus journey, for example, Lewis felt the power of his mother's example in demanding civil rights.

He remembers, "Mother was fearless in her desire that justice was done. From the time I was five until I was fifteen, as soon as school was out, my mother and I would travel by bus from New York to a farm in Virginia where her family lived. When we crossed the state line in Virginia, she would be told that we had to move to the back of the bus. My mother would say, 'I'm not going to do that.' And she stayed where she was."

Lewis regards his mother's conviction as a legacy from her mother, noting, "It was a trait that permeated my mother's family in Virginia." He recalls the leadership of his grandmother and eleven-year-old cousin Susannah in the civil rights movement in Virginia. He refers to these three women as "my sheros." "My grandmother lived in Prince Edward County, where she was a tireless supporter of the NAACP [the National Association for the Advancement of Colored People]. She was the money person," notes Lewis. Here Susannah took on a leadership role and organized a student boycott against her segregated school.

As Lewis explains, "My cousin led her classmates out of the school. For this, she was vilified and threatened. My grandmother took her in and offered her protection. Finally, we had to send Susannah to Alabama. That's when Thurgood Marshall [attorney for the NAACP] came to Virginia. And when the Supreme Court made the decision in 1954 to outlaw school segregation, Prince Edward County was one of the five counties that were part of the *Brown v. Board of Education* decision."

Lewis has artfully applied these lessons in leadership in two recent acts of conviction. First, he organized a large coalition of business leaders in New York City to speak out against the brutal sexual assault of Abner Louima, a young Haitian man, by Brooklyn police officers. Joining former New York City mayor David Dinkins and other prominent African Americans, he sponsored and signed a full-page protest ad in the *New York Times*.

Lewis describes his reaction to meeting with Louima: "Our conversation just fueled my desire to make sure nothing like that happens to any American. To the degree I can have an impact on addressing the issue of police brutality, I want to go on record stating that we don't do that to any human being."

A second scenario: last year, Lewis canceled the highly successful Essence Festival in New Orleans when he learned that Murphy J. Foster, the governor of Louisiana, had decided to eliminate all of the state's affirmative action programs. Following a flurry of phone calls, Lewis met with Governor Foster, who then issued a new executive order reinstating affirmative action.

For Lewis, the opportunity cost of relying on his inner authority and conveying his conviction was high. Yet his assessment reveals how he has organized and transformed his family template—the courage to speak out for social justice—in his own terms. Lewis says, "Even though the governor reversed his position, because of the timing I could not promote the festival. We lost several million dollars. But I thought the issue of affirmative action was extremely important, and I put my company on the line to take a stand."

Lewis offers a final striking snapshot of the full circle of his conviction. After he returned to the University of New Mexico to accept the Zimmerman Award for Outstanding Alumni, he located and visited eighty-five-year-old Howard Methany, a former dean of students who had championed Lewis after he lost his football scholarship at the end of his freshman year. Recalling how Lewis had been one of five blacks out of 8,000 students, Methany told him, "You know why you lost your scholarship? It's because you wore dashikis, you were a supporter of Malcolm X, and you made people uncomfortable."

Lewis's reaction embodies his self-consistency: "I learned that you should never give up when you embark on something. If I lost my scholarship because of my support of Malcolm X, it confirms that I am an individual who stands up for what he believes."

Calibrating Consistency

Like Fred Rogers and Leroy Hood, Ed Lewis's leadership is disciplined by self-consistency and directed by inner authority. Still, these aspects of conviction can be distinguished from two inevitable—but wrongheaded—interpretations. For these leaders, conviction is neither the ebullient Frank Sinatra singing "I Did It My Way" nor the obnoxious drill sergeant snarling, "My way, or the highway." It requires a delicate calibration between the individual and the organization.

Psychologist Prescott Lecky examined this tension between the group and the individual and believed that all behavior was motivated by the need for self-consistency and unity. For Lecky, a leader's inner work of developing meaningful convictions posed two sets of problems: the leader's problem of maintaining an inner harmony with himself or herself and then maintaining harmony with his or her environment.[9]

Ed Lewis, along with every other leader we have described, resolves this conflict by translating his individual acts of conviction into institutional values. Leroy Hood's priority of public education and Fred Rogers's insistence on authenticity suggest that when a leader's idée fixe is communicated to members of an organization, it generates tremendous power.[10]

Dave Duffield, CEO of PeopleSoft takes this point one step further by crafting a corporate culture based on his unconventional conviction.

Dave Duffield, Chairman, CEO, and President, PeopleSoft: Conviction as Culture

"If you are not having fun, go work for someone else," says chairman Dave Duffield, in a crisp summary of how his conviction shapes the corporate culture of PeopleSoft. Based in Pleasantville, California, PeopleSoft sells high-ticket, bet-your-business software that helps organizations run their human resources, accounting, and manufacturing functions. In its software war with California's Oracle and Germany's SAP to capture a $6 billion market, People-Soft boasts of a 100 percent growth each year, a 99 percent customer renewal rate, and the lowest employee turnover rate—3 percent—in Silicon Valley.[11] We found a clear connection between the high growth and low turnover in the legacy of Duffield's conviction about having fun.

Duffield, an IBM employee in the 1960s, had already succeeded in founding two software companies, Information Associated and Integral Systems, Inc., when he mortgaged his home to start People-Soft. His determination to create a fun-loving, customer-focused culture at PeopleSoft is the result of a powerful event of knowing in his leadership of Integral Systems.

"The reason I put fun in the original operating principles of PeopleSoft is that I didn't have fun at my previous company," explained Duffield. "It was full of talented personalities who became protective of their turf after they gained a certain position. People were using their energy to fight each other, rather than the competition. It became a real drag."

Duffield's event of knowing generated a new commitment. "I wasn't smart enough to know how to stop that—to change the culture—because these people were vital to the organization," he admits. His solution was "to stop dealing with these warring factions and turn the company over to someone else. When I started PeopleSoft, I was determined to keep bad behavior from entering the company. I would keep the virus out, instead of dealing with it once it infiltrated the company."

From the start, Duffield knew that having fun, while taking the customer seriously, was key to the company he wanted to create. And he knew that he had to lead by example. One route was compiling a list of optimal business behaviors he called "Dave's Rules." They begin with Rule no. 1: "Keep the restrooms clean." He explains his mirthful message: "If we can't keep the bathrooms clean, how can our customers possibly expect us to develop quality software products?"

Employees have responded to Duffield's good humor by creating an in-house band called the Raving Daves. A former bass player in college, Duffield jammed with the band at a companywide meeting at Lake Tahoe. "I think the band fits well into the culture of our company," says Duffield, who purchased more than $50,000 worth of new instruments and sound equipment for the band.

Consider, too, PeopleSoft's slapstick quarterly meetings. They are modeled after *The David Letterman Show,* with Duffield as host, and feature a comic monologue, a top-ten list, and guest appearances by clients. One guest, Microsoft's president Steve Ballmer, brought down the house when host Duffield facetiously announced a partnership with rival Oracle. Ballmer rose from the audience and delivered a memorable rant on the importance of Microsoft's relationship with PeopleSoft.

For Duffield, a second element of banishing bad behavior and maintaining a playful workplace is to avoid the trappings of hierarchy by being accessible to employees and customers. With a wisdom won in surviving the turf wars at Integral Systems, Duffield created a four-person operating committee to run the company with him and rerouted his recruiting. As he explains, "When you hire hierarchical people, you are going to have a hierarchical company. So our objective at PeopleSoft is to hire team players that are cross-functional, who will make decisions not just for the good of their department but for the good of the company. I want a manager for Latin America who could vote for adding people to the French team, rather than his own."

Leading by consistent example, Duffield hijacked corporate hierarchy by becoming what one manager calls "one of the most approachable guys on the planet" and by refusing the perks of power. This CEO works in a cubicle, answers his own phone, tracks his appointments, and types his memos. He does not have a secretary. "They tend to filter information and protect the individual," says Duffield.

His availability to customers is the stuff of corporate legends. In one meeting, he gave out his e-mail address to 7,000 customers, and he personally visits clients to fix a bug in their systems. He proudly repeats a story about the time a potential mega-client was weighing the choice of working with Oracle or PeopleSoft. Unable to cut through the hierarchy surrounding Oracle's CEO, Larry Ellison, the client called Dave Duffield, who answered his own phone and landed the business.

A final factor in Duffield's consistent conviction about fun—and driving bad behavior from the company—is a ban on office politics. As Dave's Rule no. 4 puts it, "Don't kiss up and slap down." He had no hesitation about firing an employee who was "very likeable and business-oriented with me and a tyrant with the people who worked for her."

Here is Duffield's playful but serious warning: "I don't like to see people play Jacqueline Kennedy Onassis with their boss and Atilla the Hun with the people they manage. I expect people to treat fellow employees, customers, or the bagel delivery people with the same respect and courtesy you would have offered to the late Jerry Garcia."

Pericles' Prescription

Dave Duffield might be surprised to learn that his formula for creating a corporate culture is more than 2,000 years old. Pericles, the producer of Athens's Golden Age, is widely believed to be the first leader to articulate the balance between the individual and the organization.[12] Pericles' policies are credited with perfecting Athenian democracy and generating the first public funding for architecture. We might argue that he also destroyed Athens by funding his purpose through raiding neighboring Sparta's treasury, thus sparking the Peloponnesian Wars. Still, his success can be linked to his understanding and strategic communication of what can best be understood as the "organizational culture" of Athens.

Pericles' prescription for conveying a culture's convictions is found in his famous funeral oration, delivered in 430 B.C., early in the Peloponnesian Wars. In his speech, he suggests that a thriving organizational culture requires a leader who can do two things: understand what makes the organization unique and be able to communicate the difference.

Pericles' strategy was to sketch the aspects that made Athens special—its democratic ideals and respect for each person's ability—and to remind the people that Athens was an innovation that "does not copy the institutions of our neighbors." He then skillfully summed up the balance between the individual and the organization, saying, "Here, each individual is interested not only in his own affairs, but in the affairs of the state as well. You should fix your eyes on the greatness of Athens and fall in love with her."

Similarly, much of Dave Duffield's success as a leader relies on Pericles' ancient model of understanding and communicating the unique creation of a culture. In fact, Duffield's habit of mind—his clarity about communicating PeopleSoft's culture—has generated a self-fulfilling prophecy. As he explains, "We have a reputation as kind of a loopy culture. So if you are an aggressive, don't-care-about-other-people's-feelings type, you are not going to be attracted to this company because it's not your style. The perception of us in the marketplace keeps bad behavior from entering the workplace and attracts the kind of people we want."

Yet not every leader can start and shape an organization's culture grounded in his or her own conviction. An act of inner authority may not resonate with its audience. As the next two leaders demonstrate, conviction is a habit of mind that demands personal courage.

Once again, the Greeks had a word for it—*arete*. Translation: the integrity to do what needs to be done.

Francesca Zambello, International Opera Director: The Best Judge of Your Work

Francesca Zambello's audacious productions at Paris's Bastille Opera, London's Covent Garden, Venice's Teatro la Fenice, and the Seattle and Houston Operas have fueled her reputation as the hottest, most controversial opera director of her generation.[13] Zambello deftly defines her inner authority—"the most important critic is inside of yourself"—and then offers as a case in point—an infamous night at the opera.

"It isn't fun being booed; but sometimes, it is also a badge of success," says Zambello about the opening night when she drew catcalls from New York City's Metropolitan Opera audience for her coffin-strewn staging of Donizetti's romantic *Lucia di Lammermoor*. She continues, "At the time it happened, I was completely traumatized; but then I snapped out of it. Because I realized that being an artist means that you are somebody who has a point of view. You have to live to your point of view; you can't be afraid of it."

Although Zambello has not received another contract with the Metropolitan Opera, that night was an event of knowing. She says, "It taught me that if you stick to your convictions, eventually things will come around." In fact, when the sound of booing was heard across the ocean, it generated career-making European engagements for Zambello. As she explains, "In Europe, being booed and being controversial is a positive thing. People said, 'This is interesting; this is different. Let's find out about it by hiring her to do a show.'"

Thus, in Europe and America, Zambello continued her stunning stagings. Imagine, for example, her direction of Melville's seasick story *Billy Budd* for the Houston Opera with "no boat and no uniforms" and a climactic hanging of the title character. She was not surprised when her mother saw someone reading a newspaper column titled "The Sick Mind of Zambello."

Her mother, a concert pianist, offered Zambello her first model of an independent artist. Lacking a babysitter, her mother often brought four-year-old Francesca to the theater. There Francesca would sit with the stage manager and watch the whole concert. When Francesca became a director at a young age, "inventing little scripts and dragging everyone from the neighborhood into costumes," her mother encouraged Zambello's inner authority. She urged her to "be a thinker, a creator, a performer—not to go by what the book says."

Her mother's message was echoed in the two exemplars Francesca met in her twenties: Jean Pierre Ponnelle, director of Milan's La Scala Opera, and Gilbert Hemsley, director of the New York City Opera. From each of them, Zambello received an assistant director job and an unmistakable invitation to rely on her own ability.

She recalls Gilbert Hemsley as a man who combined his artistry with giving a young person self-regard. "When I was scared about doing a job, and Gilbert would say, 'You've *got* it, girl; now go and do it!' Even today, his words always ring in my ear. He taught me about believing in myself and sticking to my convictions," she says. Both Hemsley and Ponnelle underlined Zambello's authority, providing unforgettable lessons in leadership.

Both exemplars surrounded themselves with talented people and offered them responsibility, engaging them in a peer level rather than a student-teacher level. "Jean Pierre told me, when I started to work for him at La Scala in Milan, that the reason he hired me was because he knew I would be a good director, not that I would be a good assistant," says Zambello. "His words always stick with me, because whenever I hire an assistant, I try to hire someone whom I think has potential to be a good director."

Whether Zambello is leading artists or directors-to-be, she finds a balance between collaboration and conviction. "Leadership in the theater is about collaboration, about having people invest in it personally by expressing their thoughts, ideas, and feelings. Performers often need to do their best work in a kind of tunnel. But as a director, my job is to see the big picture," she says.

One way Zambello keeps her eye on the big picture is by withholding power from the press and not reading her reviews. "A writer is only one point of view of the 2,000 people sitting in the audience," opines Zambello, who urges performers to develop an inner authority about their performances. "I want to create an environment where people feel they can be better than they ever could have possibly dreamed of."

By encouraging artists and technicians to believe in themselves and the people they respect, Zambello conveys her conviction as a habit of mind. She tells them, "The best judge of your work is ultimately yourself, and when you discover something in yourself, you must hold on to it because it's the kind of knowledge nobody else can give you. You can only teach it and learn it by yourself."

Like Francesca Zambello, Senator Paul Wellstone's conviction is a habit of mind grounded by an inner authority. A political science professor who became a politician, he has established his authority through a consistent purpose.

Senator Paul Wellstone (D-Minnesota): A Conscience of the Senate

"I have never understood why people work so hard to get into the Senate and then cast votes they don't believe in," says Minnesota senator Paul Wellstone, who has been called "a conscience in the Senate."[14] In a career defined by his consistent conviction, Wellstone's legislative agenda is not the stuff of sound bites: rekindling public interest in poverty, domestic violence, and affordable education; strengthening mental health coverage; and slashing campaign spending.

As a freshman senator, elected after twenty years as a political science professor, Wellstone relied on his inner authority and voted against the popular Persian Gulf War. He donated his pay raise to help combat domestic violence, and retraced Bobby Kennedy's trip to the Mississippi Delta to "put a human face on poverty." One term later, he was the only Democratic senator up for reelection who bucked the new congressional majority in 1996 and voted against the popular welfare reform bill, because he believed it would "put one million more children in poverty."

Wellstone's unapologetic purpose as a senator moved an astonished pundit to sum up his re-election campaign—one where his opponent Rudy Boschwitz spent $2 million in ads lambasting his liberalism—in this way: "Minnesota shamed the nation with its 67 percent turnout and wrote the story [of Paul Wellstone] that goes against the world-weariness and cynicism being dispensed elsewhere: be yourself, vote your convictions and get re-elected."[15]

Senator Wellstone has been both a student and a teacher of conviction. Intrigued with answering our questions about his legacy, he says, "In my twenty years of teaching at Carleton College, I used to give take-home exams and ask each student, 'Why do you think about politics the way you do?' Now, that is the question you are asking me."

In his answers, the legacy of his habit of mind of conviction could be mapped from his family, to his tenure fight while on the Carleton College faculty, and to his leadership on the floor of the U.S. Senate. Raised in Washington, D.C., Wellstone began to trace his family template by describing his mother, who worked in a school cafeteria. He recalls, "Her supreme compliment was to call someone a hard worker. I think my whole focus on working families and working-class issues came from her." From his father, a Jewish immigrant from the Ukraine who came to the United States "one step ahead of the pogroms," he learned to cherish education, equal justice, and freedom of expression.

Wellstone's father was a literate, multilingual man whose day job in government work paid the bills and whose night work— writing plays or essays on economics—expressed his passion. Wellstone remembers, "My father was fifty years old when I was born. As a kid, I was embarrassed by his old-country looks and actions. But when I got to high school, I realized what a treasure he was. Then every school night, at ten o'clock, we would meet in the kitchen for tea and sponge cake. He would talk about the world, and I would listen."

In the night kitchen, Wellstone learned about his father's experience as a Jew in czarist Russia. "He emphasized freedom of speech, especially the right to dissent and the importance of having the courage to speak up for what you believe in. There was a very strong emphasis on the underdog. I think my parents really did believe that the prophetic tradition of Judaism means that to love God is to love justice," says Wellstone.

Yet several years before these conversations, eleven-year-old Wellstone had witnessed the mental breakdown of his older brother, Stephen, and the unjust treatment of people with mental illness. "I remember visiting my brother in a Virginia State mental institute and seeing the people warehoused, sitting on benches, and not getting any help. I remember being so angry as a kid, thinking, 'This is so horrible; this is my *brother*,' " he says.

Wellstone calls his moment of meaning a "radicalizing experience," one that includes the knowledge of how medical bills can devastate a family. "It took my parents twenty years to pay off the hospital bills," says Wellstone. As a senator, Wellstone has been able to translate the legacy of his family's struggle into a commitment to end discrimination against mental illness. He worked for four years with Republican senator Pete Domenici of New Mexico to pass a bill to strengthen mental health coverage in health insurance plans. When the bill was signed into law, Wellstone sent the ceremonial signing pen to his brother, Stephen.

An equally powerful moment of meaning took place at Carleton College in Minnesota when Wellstone was fired for political and community activism and then—following a groundswell of student support—rehired to become, at age 27, the youngest tenured faculty member in the college's history.

Wellstone describes this event of knowing as "a sobering experience" that helped him realize why, as a community organizer, he couldn't always get people to speak up when they feared losing their jobs or homes. "It gave me more determination as a teacher, but as the father of two small children I felt guilty and worried about how I would support my family. This gave me a real sense of why some people are more interested in making a living than making history," he says.

Yet the commitment that Wellstone created at Carleton College became part of the legacy of "conscience" that he brought to the U.S. Senate. He explains, "Being able to win that struggle made me more confident about the importance of standing up for what you believe, being proud of yourself—and not being afraid to take on people with power."

In the Senate, Wellstone continues to use his pride in taking measure of his convictions. He describes how this works by confessing to one fascinating exception: his first-term yea vote about a Gulf War victory parade resolution that barred parade goers from carrying the flag of a terrorist country. "Even though I believed in the right to free assembly, I would have been the only one to vote no. So I voted the other way, and I was miserable. I was up nights; I didn't feel vital or proud. I realized that I am more effective when I'm credible to myself. It gives me drive, determination, and pride," he says.

In hot and sticky Minnesota summers, when Wellstone travels the state to seek out his constituents, they want to talk about his convictions. "Voters tell me, 'We really respect you for standing up for what you believe in, even when we don't agree with you,' " Wellstone says. "And I don't ever want to go back on that. I feel it's what I promise people."

The Self Same

We cannot imagine a more astute observer of the inner work of leaders in crafting consistent conviction than William Shakespeare. Whether portraying King Lear's purpose in passing power to his daughters or Othello's trusting Iago instead of his inner authority, Shakespeare reveals the hidden habits of mind of his characters.[16] Classics scholar Harold Bloom believes this "internalization of the self" is Shakespeare's greatest invention and notes that Shakespeare's phrase for the self was "the self same."

Recall the famously depressed Danish prince, Hamlet, who describes his inner work when he says, "I have within [myself] which passes show."[17] Yet Hamlet's purpose is too appalling—be it murderous revenge or abandoning Ophelia—for us to admire his leadership. Clearly his grief allows him to be misled by a ghost. And it is striking to realize that although Shakespeare wrote seven soliloquies for Hamlet, it is Polonius, the king's chief counselor and father of the much-lamented Ophelia, who describes the inner work of crafting conviction.

In the first act, Polonius offers his son, Laertes, the family formula for conviction as a habit of mind: "This above all: to thine own self be true. And it must follow, as the night the day; thou canst not then be false to any man."[18]

Shakespeare's phrase *the self same* and the counsel of Polonius capture the consistent conviction of the unique leaders we have described: Fred Rogers daring children to be themselves, Leroy Hood bringing science to the public, Paul Wellstone voting his conscience, and Francesca Zambello staging her nights at the opera. Borne in each leader's legacy, their conviction is "the pass that shows." Conviction makes each of them the author of their leadership.

NOTEBOOK: CONVICTION

To producer Fred Rogers, a central purpose of children's television programming is to communicate to children the kind of unconditional acceptance modeled by his grandfather on the farm.

- Describe the purpose of your work. How does your organization contribute to the lives of its customers or clients and to the strength of your community?

- What are the experiences and relationships that have influenced the sense of purpose you bring to your leadership?

Senator Paul Wellstone acknowledged the influence of his father and of his firing from Carleton College in underlining the importance of standing up for what he believes.

- Give an example of a conviction drawn from an event of knowing, a parent, or an exemplar that has been translated into a habit of mind in your leadership.

- Describe a recent situation where you offered your staff or team a model of standing up for your consistent convictions.

PeopleSoft CEO Dave Duffield crafted a fun-loving, customer-centered culture to counter the "bad behavior" of his previous start-up company.

- Identify an organizational value in a previous work setting that was at odds with your own convictions. What steps have you taken in your current organization to avoid this conflict?

- Imagine that you are beginning a new organization. Based on your past experiences, describe the convictions you would draw upon to create a new corporate culture.

Opera director Francesca Zambello defined inner authority by saying, "Sometimes the most important critic is inside yourself."

- Specify the people and experiences that offer an example of trusting, valuing, and speaking from your own experience.

- How do you (or can you) encourage people in your organization to rely on their inner authority?

Chapter 8

Replenishment

Restoring Perspective

W hen Sara Lee Corporation donated its $100 million Impressionist art collection to museums around the country, CEO and Chairman John Bryan gave up the paintings by Henri Matisse, Edgar Degas, and Camille Pissarro that hung in his executive offices in Chicago. Bryan's gift to museums—including the Metropolitan Museum in New York, the Art Institute of Chicago, and the Lauren Rogers Museum of Art in Laurel, Mississippi—creates the possibility that a wider public can use art as Bryan does.[1] For him, the "thrilling experience" of going to a museum is a source of replenishment that provides counterpoint to the demands of his work.

Bryan's artistic interests are a key to his legacy as a leader. His interest in art focuses his past experiences to define and reinvigorate his leadership. Listening to John Bryan, who has acquired more than 120 companies while at the helm of Sara Lee, we understand how leaders draw upon the resource of replenishment as a powerful habit of mind to restore their perspective.

In exploring this fifth and final habit of mind, we offer a series of short scenarios to describe the way several leaders—ones we have introduced in earlier chapters—think about and manage their time away from work. Replenishment involves each leader in the craft of counterpoint. They use their private lives to create a different sense of self, a different sense of purpose, or a different sense of time in contrast to the demands of their leadership.

In their stories, we see the paradox of replenishment and how it employs personal habits driven by a habit of mind. Through replenishment, leaders make thoughtful choices about life away from work. They can also renew the richness of the other habits of mind we have described in earlier chapters. John Bryan offers a finely detailed portrait of this process.

A Clear Perspective

When John Bryan was ten years old, he didn't know much about art; but he knew what he liked. He says, "Between ages 10 and 12, I started making aesthetic judgments around the house and began to tell my mother and sister what to wear. I started to move the furniture around. When we built a house, I contributed some architectural changes. There were no museums within 150 miles of where I lived, but it was pretty obvious that I was running around and looking at things."

The legacy of Bryan's childhood experiences with art found its first corporate expression when Sara Lee began buying Impressionist paintings and sculpture in the 1980s. The collection grew as a means of associating the company with quality and then as a tribute to Bryan's exemplar, Nathan Cummings, the founder of Sara Lee's predecessor company, Consolidated Foods, who had once owned all of the artworks.

Bryan remembers, "Nate Cummings introduced me to the fine art world. I started going with him to galleries and then when he started to sell some of his own art, I bought some of the pieces and started a collection at Sara Lee that once was a major focus of the cultural world. I was conditioned to be a business person, and it took me a while to weave the arts into my working life. But even if I hadn't met Nate, I would still have been interested."

In fact, Bryan's continued artistic interests in his private as well as professional life creates a means of replenishment. He describes how art offers a different sense of self and purpose: "I've visited gardens and museums around the world. I've created a lot of spaces and developed a lot of collections. I play with those on weekends. Some people like to fish or hunt, or ski or boat—everybody's got their own thing. Mine is the garden, the architecture, the landscape, the collections in the main house. I see this both as being creative—

doing something with your time that has meaning—but also as creating something that hasn't been done before."

Bryan also explains how these mindful choices replenish his strength as a leader by creating a different sense of time. "I think it puts things in perspective," says Bryan. "If you look at the fast-changing business world, art is the only thing that lasts forever. I can get enraptured by looking at fine arts and decorative arts. It's been a marvelous counterpoint to grinding out all of the risks, the tough choices, and confrontations in the business world."

Whether he is home in Chicago or traveling around the globe, Bryan knows how to leave the office behind. "I don't carry the pressures home with me; I pick up an art book or run through the landscape, or think about my collections. I don't travel anywhere where I don't stop by a museum or gallery. I know so many people who go to New York once a month. They get off a plane, fight traffic, go to a hotel for a terrible meeting, and come back. You know, I'll run by the Metropolitan Museum. . . ."

The Art of Replenishment

John Bryan's reliance on fine art to freshen his perspective recalls MetLife Chairman and CEO Harry Kamen's experience with music, as described in the introduction. Like Bryan, Kamen's legacy linked an early encounter with the arts—attending the Metropolitan Opera—with his later professional and personal connection with the arts. Kamen offers corporate and financial support for Lincoln Center and uses music as his replenishment. "A Mozart or Schubert quartet can bring tears to my eyes, I find this experience of music clears the mind and psyche and get me ready for the next day," he says.

Both of these leaders appear to be drawing upon the counsel of a legendary Renaissance leader. In his *Treatise on Painting*, Leonardo da Vinci advises, "It is well that you should leave off work and take a little relaxation because when you come back to it you are a better judge." Da Vinci was convinced that time away from work was key to gaining perspective and to incubating and generating new ideas.[2]

This idea did not always amuse his patrons. Art historian Giorgio Vasari reveals that when Leonardo was working on *The Last Supper*, he would paint for days on the scaffold from morning till night and then, without warning, take a long break. Vasari wrote, "To the Prior of Santa Maria delle Grazie, it seemed strange that Leonardo sometimes spent half the day lost in thought. When the Prior complained to the Duke, Leonardo persuaded his royal patron that the greatest geniuses sometimes accomplish more when they work less."[3]

Many leaders understand and practice Leonardo's art of incubation, accomplishing more through the practice of replenishment. For example, Beckie Masaki, executive director of the Asian Women's Shelter in San Francisco, has translated her legacy as a visual artist into a mindful approach to replenishment.

Beckie Masaki, Executive Director, Asian Women's Shelter: Other Realms to Replenish

Several years ago, when Beckie Masaki took a two-month sabbatical, she traveled to the Windcall Institute, a retreat center in Montana. She describes Windcall as a retreat for "burned-out activists," a place where she "refound my artist strand and filled the walls of their art studio." Prior to her leadership in the domestic violence field, Masaki had worked primarily as a visual artist, creating prints, collage, and mixed-media pieces that often reflected Japanese tradition. For Masaki, the art that filled the walls of Windcall was a reminder "to see the importance of creative outlets and the potential of beauty to replenish the self."

Masaki's struggle to integrate her love of art with her commitment to social activism is central to the way she draws upon replenishment as a habit of mind. As she explains, "We give so much on our jobs, but we can't be martyrs. Our work is rewarding, but we must find other realms to replenish and strengthen ourselves. If we don't, we are not practicing the message we give other people, which is to take care of yourself. The challenge for me, since I can't devote long pieces of solitary time to being an artist, is to find other ways to use my free time to support and participate in the arts in a different way."

The different ways Masaki replenishes with art include taking time for an occasional large-scale project. For example, a mixed-media piece about a grandmother she never knew was displayed at San Francisco's Mission Cultural Center. More often, she describes her connection with art as "little projects": creating notecards and a mural for the shelter, taking jazz and salsa dance classes, and attending arts performances with friends and family. The work of other women artists and writers—especially those artists who use culture and art for social change, such as Maya Angelou, Alice Walker, and Jessica Hagedorn—captivate her.[4]

Masaki is clear about how her involvement in the arts refocuses her purpose in her work. "When you are involved with art, you are an observer of the world. Being able to communicate or express in a different mode triggers my own creativity to step back and see my work at the shelter from a different perspective," she says. "Although art does not get at the daily injustices, artistic images speak to what I hope for the world: that we can rebuild a more whole connection to our culture and community."

Counterpoint

Replenishment is the habit of mind of thinking about counterpoint. It must not be confused with the clichéd concept of "balance"; it cannot hint at the antiquated idea of "having it all." When leaders make thoughtful choices about using private time to create a different sense of self, purpose, and time, they experience different and restorative satisfactions than the mastery of their jobs.

Replenishment is a study in contrasts. Recall that John Bryan describes his passionate patronage of the arts as "a marvelous counterpoint to grinding out all of the risks" in the business world. Consider how Beckie Masaki's return to her involvement in the arts counterbalances and reenergizes her involvement as a social activist. Then examine opera director Francesca Zambello's mirror-opposite pattern of replenishment. Her time away from her artistry refreshes her reality as a leader.

Francesca Zambello, International Opera Director: Creating Contrast

Francesca Zambello explains why counterpoint is the key to replenishment. "You must have something away from your work to understand your work," she says. "Unless you have another world your mind can exist in, you cannot be refreshed when you return to the world where you are supposed to be a leader."

The legacy of this lesson was a moment of meaning following Zambello's loss of her cherished exemplars, opera directors Jean Pierre Ponnelle and Gilbert Hemsley. She told us, "My twenties were spent like most people—working at top pace, not taking care of myself. Then in my thirties, when so many friends died of AIDs, I realized that I needed to have a base and a grounding—to take time to appreciate and cherish the life I had. A great loss precipitated that realization for me," she says.

For Zambello, the key to her "grounding" was beginning a decade-long loving relationship and making deliberate choices to counterpoint the pace of her work with the practice of self-renewal. Noting that her replenishments are "incredibly mundane," she says, "I work at a very hectic pace; I travel so often. So I like to stay at home or go to our nearby house in the country. Being at home is grounding because I do all the things I want to do but I don't have time for: reading books, seeing movies, or just quietly petting the dog."

Her definition of replenishment captures the essence of its counterpoint: "I have a million-dollar budget on my back every time I do a show. So I think you need to have a world where the other part of your spirit is replenished. Then you can come back and lead the forces. You only get better by having the contrast in your life," Zambello says.

The contrast, or counterpoint, Zambello describes is sought by many leaders in the presence of family.

Neil Austrian, President and COO, National Football League: Family as Oasis

When Neil Austrian was offered the job as president of the National Football League, he told the board, "If you think I am going to be one of those guys who works every Sunday, you've got the wrong guy. I have a really strong commitment to spending time with my family." As the NFL's President, Austrian runs an organization that provides millions of fans with replenishment, or what Austrian calls "a diversion in their lives." But for Austrian, his family is his source of replenishment. "They are an oasis from the chaos of my job," he says.

Austrian's focus on his family can be linked to a moment of meaning in conversation with an early boss in the investment banking business. On a field trip to Delaware, the soon-to-be-retired chairman of Laird Inc. told Austrian, "Don't make the same mistake I did. Get to know your family and spend time with them." Austrian looks back at this advice as "a defining experience." He says, "Listening to this guy, it was clear that although he had a great career, he was pretty unhappy with himself and his family life—wishing it could be different."

For Austrian, the event of knowing yielded a fresh commitment. As he explains, "I came from a close family, so I knew about the importance of family life. But I was twenty-eight years old, just out of graduate school, when I realized that I didn't want to be in his shoes, at age 65, giving the same advice to someone else." In fact, Austrian now advises employees, "If you do the job right, you can put your family first."

Yet Austrian understands that simply spending more time at home is not the key to a replenishing family life. Creating an oasis from his job's chaos is a counterpoint to his leadership of the NFL. The father of six children, three adopted at older ages, he is moved by the excitement of "getting involved in the issues in my children's lives that are not my issues—that have absolutely nothing to do with business." He will fly all night to arrive home in time to coach a lacrosse game or applaud at a school play.

Austrian describes these involvements as "more important than my job" and adds, "Because these events are important to my kids, they become important to me. It puts my business in perspective. I will always remember teaching my daughter to ski as opposed to the deal I was making at the time."

Still, because Austrian presides over a competitive sport and where every minute of his day is scheduled, he goes one step further in protecting his family time from the pressures of his work. He says, "I played competitive sports in college; I'm in a competitive business. So I don't want to compete over the weekend. I play golf and sail, but when I play golf, I play with my wife, Nancy. We play nine holes and take one of the kids to drive the cart; so we spend time with them."

Austrian refuses to sail competitively. He prefers to day sail with the family or charters a boat for a family vacation. And he creates a different sense of time by refusing to have an agenda or an itinerary. Instead, his approach to his family creates a counterpoint to his overflowing Filofax. He asks them, "What do you guys want to do today?"

A Habit of Mind

Neil Austrian's approach to replenishment as a habit of mind allows him to energize his performance and to keep pressure from undermining his leadership. By protecting his family time from the demands of leading the NFL, Austrian experiences a different sense of time and self. By avoiding the trap of working hard and playing hard, he is able to recover from career demands and revitalize his leadership.

Austrian's habit of thinking about life after work as a source of replenishment is an approach common to dozens of leaders we interviewed. In questioning them, we found the expected routes to renewal: skiing, scuba diving, mountaineering, music, painting, religious worship, voracious reading, faraway places, and community service. And we found the unexpected: Roosevelt Bank COO Anat Bird was once invited to be a guest chef at the legendary Le Cirque restaurant in New York City. Bird buys chocolate in 10-kilogram chunks and finds replenishment in baking more than eighty birthday cakes a year for her employees.

Yet all of these replenishing activities are driven by a similar way of thinking about leadership. Al Gamper, CEO of the CIT Financial Group, maps the way it works.

Al Gamper, CEO, CIT Financial Group: Get Involved outside the Job

CIT Financial Group CEO Al Gamper reveals how replenishment operates as a habit of mind: "I have to carry CIT twenty-four hours a day, but I manage to compartmentalize it by looking at other things. So I clock off when I leave here; I put CIT in a corner. I don't go home and visit CIT problems on my family. I go home to celebrate my wife's birthday, make travel plans, or attend a Rutgers University board meeting, where we are kicking around some really critical issues on the future of the university. I think this rejuvenates my ability to run CIT."

Gamper credits his father for encouraging him to "always learn something new" and his exemplar, John McGilicutty, a past chairman of Manufacturers Hanover, for urging him to "broaden yourself and get involved outside of the job." Gamper intends to translate McGilicutty's model for a new generation of leaders. He relates a smart story about lecturing at MIT's Sloan School of Business with Hisao Kabayashi, CIT's Japanese cochairman.

After Gamper's lecture, a student stood and asked him, "Mr. Gamper, are you a workaholic?" Gamper answered, "No way. I take vacations; I have many other interests." Then when the student told him that he was the first CEO who denied being a workaholic, Gamper said, "They are all bullshitting you. That's just the image they want to portray." The questioner then turned to Kabayashi, who answered, "I was a workaholic for thirty-five years, and last summer, I lost my stomach for it. I think I prefer Mr. Gamper's approach."

Replenishment is the essence of Gamper's approach. As he puts it, "You can't be so driven by your job that you spend all your resources on the job. You have to have diversity in your life. To me, diversity is the way to keep your batteries from running down."

A final story suggests how a banking executive draws upon her unique legacy to recharge her batteries and revitalize her leadership.

Phyllis Campbell, President, U.S. Bank of Washington: "Stop Playing the Flute"

As a young child, U.S. Bank of Washington's president, Phyllis Campbell, was fascinated by her grandfather, Tomotsu Sebastian Takizaki. He was the owner of a small grocery and antique store and a collector of fine art whose friends included painters Mark Tobey and Paul Horiuchi.[5] Campbell says, "I remember him sitting on a couch with his arms folded across his chest. We all thought that he was sleeping. But he was meditating, looking at an art object. No one talked to him, and I always wondered what he was thinking. How could he just sit there for hours?"

As a teenager, Campbell read an interview with her grandfather in the *Seattle Times*. Here, she found a story that revealed some of her grandfather's unspoken thoughts. Over the years, it became a guiding metaphor for her own practice of replenishment.

The story focused on a flutist, one who did little but practice his flute. When his playing did not improve, he sought Grandpa Takizaki's advice. Takizaki told him to stop playing the flute and find ways to help his friends and neighbors. Many weeks later, the man called to thank him for the advice and to report that his playing was much improved.

Campbell's reaction to the story evolved over the years. She explains, "When I read the story as a kid, I thought it was a silly story. But as I got older, the more I thought about it, the story became a metaphor for me. Because I am so task oriented, I tend to lose the forest for the trees. When I can step outside of myself, like in the story, and see there is a lot more out there, things happen the way they need to happen. I'm thankful for that story, and I've told it several times in my leadership."

Campbell has translated her grandfather's advice about seeking a different sense of self through community involvement in several unique ways. She stops "playing the flute" with daily "mini vacations" of exercise or reflective meditation and an annual personal retreat of several days. She jokes, "This is probably the last thing that a high-energy, high-people-person like me would choose to do. But I realized that one of the most important things I could do was to take a quiet retreat time for myself."

Campbell describes a paradoxical outcome of this time alone: It underlines her commitment to help friends and neighbors. She says, "One of my destinations is a silent retreat house in the middle of wooded acres run by Catholic nuns. It's an amazing place, a wonderful place to replenish and refresh. It is difficult for me to reflect, not to talk, to be silent. But a lot of my reflection is about my talents and purpose—understanding how my leadership is not just about achieving tactical goals, but it's also about bringing other people along, being considerate, and giving back to the community."

Campbell's community involvements range from chairing the local United Way Campaign and raising a record-breaking $6.8 million to serving on the boards of the Pacific Science Center, the Seattle Symphony Foundation, and Washington State University. Last year, the American Jewish Committee honored Campbell with its Human Relations Award for her civic contributions.

Campbell sums up the strategy of her grandfather's story: "Get out of yourself for a while, and see there is a lot more out there. Maybe the essential work of a leader is to expand the pie. The more we concentrate on giving back, whether it is giving a compliment or doing different things for different people, the more is available for everybody else."

Her grandfather's story of the flute—and the way Phyllis Campbell translates its wisdom in her leadership—defines replenishment in one sentence: It's the pause between the notes.

NOTEBOOK: REPLENISHMENT

Sara Lee CEO John Bryan's relationship with Nathan Cummings strengthened an interest in art that now provides Bryan with a counterpoint to "grinding out the tough choices and confrontations in the business world."

- Describe a family member or exemplar who offered a model of productivity that included replenishment or someone whose example suggested the value of working around the clock. How have you translated these models in your leadership?

- List activities that provide you with a clear counterpoint to the demands of your leadership. What gives you a different sense of self, of purpose, or of time?

For NFL President Neil Austrian, whose early boss modeled the importance of family, replenishment also involves a retreat from competition in his private life.

- Specify the ways you protect your private time with your family.

- How do you (or could you) encourage your staff or team to draw upon the replenishment of family and friends?

Inspired by her grandfather's advice to "stop playing the flute," U.S. Bank of Washington President Phyllis Campbell finds replenishment as a community volunteer.

- Describe the ways you stop "playing the flute" and seek a different sense of self through community involvement.

Replenishment was a powerful habit of mind for Leonardo da Vinci, who advised that spending time away from work was the key to gaining perspective and incubating new ideas.

- Identify the people in your organization who rely upon replenishment as a habit of mind to reinvigorate their leadership. What are the key behaviors and attitudes you observe?

- Recall a time when you—or someone on your team—took time away from a problem or project and returned to work with new ideas or a freshened perspective or a time when working too long on a task resulted in a diminished creativity. How have you applied these examples in your leadership?

Endnote

Leadership as a Habit of Mind

D r. Ruth Simmons is the great-granddaughter of slaves, the daughter of a Texas sharecropper, and the president of Smith College. She asks, "Do you know what kept me up at night when I was offered this job? It wasn't whether I could do the job—I knew I could—but I wondered, Could I take the job and still be the person my mother wanted me to be?"

We interviewed Ruth Simmons in the first summer of our research for this book, and we were not alone in our interest in Simmons's legacy as a leader. In fact, her appointment as the first African American woman to head a top-ranked college had created a clamor of questions about her life experiences.[1] Inquiring minds wanted to know: How had she traveled the distance between the cotton fields of Texas and the ivy walls of Smith?

Simmons says that when she was first named president of the college, talking about her legacy was one of the most demanding parts of the new job. "Suddenly, I was asked to publicly reflect on the lessons of my life. It was the parents and children who asked, 'How did this happen? Why are so many children trapped in circumstances like mine who do not escape?' People are looking for a formula, but there isn't one."

Ruth Simmons is right. There is no formula for inner work. Each leader must create a unique meaning about the events and relationships in the past. Ruth Simmons's legacy confirms the most compelling conclusion of our research: Leadership is not a role; it is a habit of mind—a point of view developed by creating meaning from the experiences of a lifetime.

Tracing the Family Template

The youngest of twelve children, Simmons was a keen observer of both of her parents as leaders. Each parent played a part in stimulating the development of her point of view—the habits of mind that would later define Simmons's leadership.

Simmons's father was an authoritarian figure who "made decisions about virtually everything." Although Simmons was close to her father, she understands how much he missed. "It wasn't satisfying to lead the family that way," she observes. "He didn't get the full benefit of family life and love from his children."

Simmons sums up this early lesson in leadership: "As a child, I instinctively knew that there must be ways of dealing with people and developing agreements that were more satisfying than simply saying, 'My way is the best way.' " For her, this curriculum was a corrective lesson, one that sent her looking for a different model of leadership. Over the years, guided by these insights, she was able to create a more collaborative approach.

Simmons integrated the experience of her father's rigid leadership in the development of her own convictions about being in charge. As she explains, "In the academic world, we work on building consensus. If you are a leader, you can make things happen or make the resources available. But you also know that unless you have the support of colleagues, the success will be pretty short lived."

Her father's leadership told the cautionary tale, but her mother's leadership provided the moral of the story. In the introduction, we described how Simmons's mother took her daughter to work and how Simmons leveraged the lesson of watching her mother iron and clean into a conviction about the value of being committed to her work.

Simmons also remembers a lesson from listening to her mother: "I have this image of my mother sitting around the kitchen table, shelling peas and teaching the twelve of us lessons from our forebears. She would tell the stories of people in our community—how they grew and what they did with their lives. There would always be a moral attached to the story, offering an insight into human nature or human frailty and what can happen with the missteps people make in life."

The values Simmons learned from her mother's stories—humility, respect for other people regardless of their background, and meeting your obligations—are convictions that form what she calls "the compass of her leadership at Smith." When we trace her family template, we learn how creative Simmons has been in putting her own stamp on the values she learned as a child.

We also understand what made Simmons sleepless at the prospect of leading Smith College. She wants to preserve her resource of attunement—her capacity to understand and respect the people she leads. As she explains, "Because of my background, I have this absolute fear of arrogance and losing myself in power and prestige. So I worry a lot about how I am seen by the people at the lower end of the organization. It is my checkpoint; I talk about it all the time. Whenever I am called upon to rally the community, I talk about the value of each individual and what it means for us as an institution to care and worry about each person."

Clearly, her mother's storytelling nurtured conviction and attunement as habits of mind in Ruth Simmons's leadership. This kitchen "cabinet" also became a template for the resource of reflection, teaching Simmons how to observe her own behavior and learn from her experiences. She says, "My mother built this structure in these lessons about life, and I learned some basic values in dealing with human beings. She also observed our behavior on a daily basis and corrected us when our behavior didn't correspond to the model she had in mind."

Simmons continues to reflect on her behavior. "I spend a lot of time thinking about whether I am living up to the models I set for myself. If I am not, I tend to make changes," she says. "I reflect on what I am doing. I am so conscious of whether I am making the right choices and whether those choices convey the right values."

The Baby of the Family

The legacy of Simmons's family role—her youngest-of-twelve-siblings status—is her ability to feel at home amid disagreement. Her experiences as a pint-size persuader resulted in a distinctive habit of mind, or a framework that allows her gracefully to interpret the many arguments in academia.

"With twelve children, what you basically do is quarrel all the time," Simmons recalls. "So there is a tremendous role for someone who tries to make things right. I liked the art of persuasion and developed the skills of negotiating between my parents and the other children."

Simmons explains how she brings this legacy to her leadership: "Being president of a college is very much what I did as a child. Everyone has a set of things they feel passionate about. Just imagine trying to introduce something new! So I do what I did in my family: try to build a common aim across different viewpoints and try to persuade people that there is something they can all care about," she says.

Loud voices don't trouble Simmons, because her optimistic framework for interpreting discord is a habit of mind cultivated in her childhood role. Some people find acrimony and discord unsettling, but Simmons says she feels right at home. "In some ways, I am at my best in those situations," she says. "For me, when there is noise or disagreement, something important is happening. I stay focused on the end point and tell myself, 'If we are having this much engagement, surely we will end up at a point were we understand things better.' "

Transforming the Template

Ruth Simmons has translated her observations about her parents' leadership and her role as a peacemaker to develop a distinct point of view as a leader. Like Simmons, many of the leaders we have described found both inspiration and caution within their family circle. We think of Len Riggio, who transformed his prizefighter father's openness to new ideas into a habit of mind of attunement, and Bigsby & Kruthers President Gene Silberberg, a child of Holocaust survivors, who transcended his parents' pessimism to create an optimistic framework for his leadership.

These leaders enable us to avoid the fallacy of family determinism, because our research shows that the family template contributes to—but does not cause—the creation of habits of mind. Instead, we find that exceptional leaders have done their inner homework, transforming the imprint and lessons of family into resources as distinctive as their own fingerprints.

Psychiatrist Alfred Adler sheds light on how the legacy of family is a rich source but not the sole determinant of lessons for these leaders.[2] Adler viewed every child as interactive with the world around him or her, experiencing events, making observations about what happened during those events, and drawing conclusions. These conclusions create an inner cognitive map, one that shapes the child's habits of viewing himself or herself, others, and the world at large.

Adler recognized that as children and adults we are active participants in our own development, and we are involved in shaping our point of view as opposed to being passive witnesses or victims of psychological conflict and crisis. In this light, we understand how leaders like Ruth Simmons are made and not born.

Our research also suggests that the legacy of leaders does not begin and end with the influence of family and is not completed in the earliest years of life. For many leaders, including Simmons, the nature of their inner work was layered with the influence of important people outside the family who stimulated their point of view.

The World as Teacher

The powerful influence of the world outside her family can be glimpsed in Simmons's description of two exemplars—one, encountered as a child; the other, early in her career. Both teachers' behavior was a model for developing the habits of mind that characterize Simmons's leadership.

"Miss Ida Mae," the kindergarten teacher at the all-black elementary school in Grapeland, Texas, was the first teacher Ruth Simmons had ever met. She also became her first cheerleader. As Simmons recalls, "I came from this isolated rural area and went off to school. I was untested: There was no play school, no games to understand your strengths or intelligence. I went from home to school. Then, in my very first encounter at school, I had this teacher who led me to believe, in all of her actions, that I was a bright person."

Ida Mae Henderson was a true discoverer; she nurtured Simmons by offering her a new view of herself. As Simmons puts it, "Here was this very educated and important person who said to me, 'Gee, that's good. You are a very smart girl.' Because she was so affirming, that is the stance I took in my life regarding school: 'If she says I'm smart, then I must be. Maybe I didn't have to pick cotton.' That was my introduction to school, and it set the tone for what I did thereafter."

For Simmons, school was a magical place. Throughout the day, she would race through her course work, learning "as fast as my hunger would take me." She continued to find teachers like her drama coach, Vernell Lillie, who discovered her and singled her out. "It was as if they were saying, 'If you keep on working that way, I am going to find other things for you to learn and do something special for you.' " Lillie took her to plays and the opera and became even more important after Simmons's mother died when Simmons was fifteen years old.

Simmons compares these teachers to CEOs. By "discovering" her, they offered her a model for her own strengths and an important lesson in valuing the richness of each individual in her organization. Simmons explains, "From my teachers, I learned that leading is more than following a textbook model; it also means taking your heart and soul and looking for the opportunity to do something wonderful for the people you lead."

In her leadership of Smith College, Simmons integrates these experiences into a habit of mind of attunement. She makes time to notice a student or faculty member who needs something beyond what her job requires her to do. She confesses, "I'm a rule breaker. I can't count the times people have come to me saying they need something, but rules make it impossible. So I find ways to test the rules, because part of the responsibility of being a leader is to find out if we have the right rules."

Simmons offers the example of a faculty member who wants to travel to complete exciting research but whose project doesn't fit into the technical guidelines for faculty travel. Listen to her regard for each teacher's experience: "When I can see that this person has the potential to do some of their most important work, I will find a way to get it done. If you ask me what I would like people to say about me, it would be that I actually think about people beyond the formal aspect of my job—that I don't act in my role, but look at each person and try to do something wonderful for them."

The Instructor: A Vote of Confidence

Exemplars who taught Ruth Simmons about herself as an adult played a key role in stimulating her confidence and conviction as a leader. When Simmons was associate dean at Princeton University, she enjoyed a unique relationship with the "tough and blustery" dean of faculty, Aaron Lembeck. Lembeck was an instructor who believed in Simmons, told her she would someday be president of a college, and offered her some of the toughest criticism of her life.

Simmons recalls, "Instead of simply telling me I had potential, he began to criticize my weaknesses. For the first time since I left my own African American community, I found someone who would actually tell me what was wrong instead of being patronizing or abidingly polite. Nobody had ever trusted me enough to give me the criticism I needed to become better at what I did. His comments were so painful and refreshing, and so helpful in the end. What he gave me was the confidence that I could take criticism and improve."

Lembeck's vote of confidence offered Simmons a mirror for

self-appraisal as well as a model for a conviction that she expresses in her own leadership. As she explains, "When I talk to minority students and women, I tell them about my relationship with Aaron Lembeck and urge them to get someone who will give them that kind of criticism. I feel so strongly about the value it had that I insist on doing it for other people."

The afternoon we talked to Simmons, this legacy was at work as she recalled a morning conversation with a staff member who was convinced she was running a problem-free project. Simmons says, "I told her about the difficulties I saw. And I explained that the reason I was telling her about the problems was because the most valuable help I ever got was from Aaron telling me what I needed to do to correct myself. I began by saying, 'I'm doing this because I really want to help you succeed.' "

The Blessing of Models

In detailing the influence of the world of teachers and models outside Ruth Simmons's family, we discover patterns that echo in the lives of the leaders we have described. Like Simmons, many leaders' lives were enriched by their relationship with exemplars who discovered their uniqueness and potential and created fertile models for the growth of inner resources.

We think of how UNUM CEO Steve Center became a discoverer for future UNUM president Elaine Rosen and modeled the habit of reflecting on behavior and business decisions in context. We recall dyslexic writer Steve Cannell, who met his champion in the University of Oregon writing instructor, Ralph Salisbury, and now applies Salisbury's conviction about how to "turn on the lights" for young writers. And Bill Shore uses the optimistic habit of mind of his "headmaster," Senator Gary Hart, to create a revolutionary model of fighting world hunger at Share Our Strength. We also take note of leaders whose experiences—Esther Torres's work on the farm, John Stanford's stint in the military, Tim Girvin's study of Zen Buddhism—created guiding metaphors to define their points of view.

Each leader applies the lesson from these people or experiences, translating the lesson to build powerful habits of mind. From all of these leaders, we conclude that the role of models is to bestow a blessing on the next generation of leaders, one that is spoken in each leader's unique voice.

The Moments of Meaning

Simmons describes two experiences she calls "epiphanies." Each experience dramatically altered her perspective about herself and her work; both took place on a college campus. In one, she is a young student; the other, a young educator. These experiences sharpened her habits of mind of reflection and conviction and her capacity to rely on her inner authority.

With teacher Vernell Lillie's help, Ruth Simmons won a scholarship to the all-black Dillard University in New Orleans. Later, in her junior year, she became an exchange student at the all-woman Wellesley College. Here, an event of knowing was a catalyst for her conviction and for her learning to rely on her inner authority and ability.

She explains, "I realized that I could do anything these very wealthy and well-prepared white women could do. I had sort of suspected there wasn't much to all of this hype about blacks being inferior to whites. But now I knew the truth, and an electric bolt went through me." Simmons calls the all-woman climate at Wellesley transformative. "I took ownership of my abilities. I discovered that not only could women do interesting things, but they could run things," she says.

Years later, another moment of meaning on a college campus strengthened her inner authority: Simmons accepted a job offer everyone told her to refuse. Simmons was director of students at Princeton's Butler College when she was offered the chair of the struggling, underfunded Afro-American Studies Department. She remembers, "Everybody told me that if I wanted to be successful, I shouldn't go in that direction. But this advice ignored my own motivations, my interests, my belief in myself, and willingness to put energy and creativity into it. In fact, the job played to my greatest strengths and abilities."

Simmons took the job, increased the budget, and built a program of the highest caliber with a faculty that included Nobel laureate and author of *Beloved*, Toni Morrison (who was hired only after Simmons researched and wrote Morrison's résumé, which Morrison refused to submit but the search committee insisted on seeing). Simmons considers her accomplishments in the program to have the most lasting impact of her work at Princeton, including her stint as associate faculty dean.

Simmons's decision allowed her to define the meaning of inner authority and articulate the conviction she takes to work every day: "What it taught me is to trust my own judgment about my skills and abilities. I will always seek other opinions, but I will not be afraid to risk for something I believe in. There are hundreds of times in a job like this where you can feel shaken in your ability. You have to be able to get up every day and have the confidence—no matter what you face—you can handle it."

Events of Knowing

Two illuminating moments were crucial in the development of the inner authority that grounds Simmons's conviction as a leader. As a young student at Wellesley College, she compared her ability to that of other students and experienced a life-changing glimpse of her potential. Later, at Princeton, she relied on her own judgment and succeeded in a job others saw as an arena for surefire failure. Both of these experiences encouraged Simmons to draw upon her inner authority and deepen her conviction about taking risks.

Like Simmons, the leaders we have studied were influenced by important life experiences that captured their attention and to which they attributed meaning. Convinced by the insights they gained, these leaders express their new commitment in strategic habits of mind. For example, Chicago Cubs president Andy Mac-

Phail, who made sense of his experience with a sandwich, leveraged his lesson into a resilient framework for addressing the team's successes and failures. Think also of Governor Gary Locke, who drew upon the memory and meaning of his horror at his grandmother's impoverished Hong Kong housing and developed his legislative conviction about affordable housing; and of Microsoft executive Scott Oki, whose acceptance of Mary Gates's invitation to join the Children's Hospital board led to his conviction about changing the venue of his leadership to the nonprofit arena. Each of these leaders express the meaning of significant events in the point of view they bring to their leadership.

The Invitation to Inner Work

Ruth Simmons's legacy highlights our premise that leadership is not a role, but a point of view. Born of the experiences of a lifetime, Simmons's leadership is anchored by the habits of mind that give substance and style to her stewardship at Smith College. And we concur with Simmons's conclusion that there is no formula for creating a leader.

In fact, we found that the creativity and grace of Ruth Simmons and sixty-some other leaders in translating legacy into leadership yielded neither predictions nor prescriptions. Instead, all of the leaders we have described offer an invitation: to translate your legacy into a point of view that can define your leadership.

There is a rich experience awaiting each of us by following the examples of the leaders interviewed. This inner work involves asking the following questions: What did I learn by observing my parents as leaders? Who were the exemplars that championed my ability or offered me an instructive model of leadership? What are the experiences that have offered me a model or metaphor to guide my leadership? What are the life-changing events that have shifted my perspective? And, finally, how are the lessons that I have learned from family, exemplars, experiences, and illuminating moments reflected in my habits of mind as a leader?

As you explore your own legacy as a leader, remember that Ruth Simmons taught us that personal history is not destiny. As Aldous Huxley explained, it is shaped by what you do with what happens to you. And Broadway director Dan Sullivan, whose childhood bedtime kept him from seeing the end of the movies, reminds us that legacy is just the beginning of the story. Each leader must learn to finish the story. Your legacy as a leader does not compel you simply to imitate or correct your past. It invites an act of alchemy—the creation of your unique point of view as a leader.

A Fresh Approach to Leadership Tracking

Every summer, in the Gifford Pinchot National Forest in eastern Oregon, surrounded by maple trees, salal bushes, and grapevines, 2,000 middle and high schoolers attend the Cispus Leadership Training Camp. Susan Fortin, the director of the program, describes an approach to training and developing leaders that reflects this new paradigm of inner work.[3]

"We used to think that being a leader was a set of cut-and-dried skills, like running a meeting or organizing a project," Fortin says. "Now, we focus on leading from the inside. Our counselors ask kids, 'Who are you as a person?' Because if kids can take a good look at themselves, they will think about what is right and not just what is easy. When you know yourself inside, it gives you direction. When kids know what gives them their passion, they will make the world better."

Fortin describes the connection between this inner homework of young leaders and the ability to influence others: "When you know what matters to you, you are able to think beyond yourself, to build trusting relationships, to listen, and build consensus. We talk to kids about earned versus appointed leadership. Our message: Other kids will view you as a leader because of who you are."

Similarly, when we train new leaders to develop a unique point of view, we encourage them to do this inner homework and explore the events and relationships that have influenced them. These explorations can result in some less-than-typical training scenarios. For example: A group of Coldwell Banker executives sketch stick figure portraits of their families, top Nestle managers remember grade school teachers, medical CEOs recall college mentors, and Andersen Consulting partners describe the events that have shaped their values.

When we recall the inner work of the many leaders we have studied and taught, we are impressed with how committed each person has been in developing his or her leadership from the inside out. By translating the lessons learned from his or her legacy, each leader crafts the habits of mind that define his or her leadership.

When we think about how Ruth Simmons translated her mother's kitchen table stories into a template for reflection, we also remember Cherokee chief Wilma Mankiller, whose lessons in "being of good mind" became a guiding metaphor for her resilient framework; Dr. Mitchell Rabkin, whose lunch with the custodian who swept his corridor awakened his attunement; Fred Rogers, who carried his grandfather's message of self-regard in his conviction about the potential of television; and Sara Lee CEO John Bryan, who crafted his childhood experiences with art into a career-long habit of replenishment.

Our study of the inner work of these leaders has been moving, inviting, often amusing, and always invigorating. As we explored the legacy of their leadership—and its expression in powerful habits of mind—we understood the wisdom in Søren Kierkegaard's observation: "Life is understood backward, but lived forward."

Notes

Introduction: The Inner Work of Leaders

1. The expression "habit of mind" is suggested in Martin Seligman's work on resilience, especially *Learned Optimism* (New York: Pocket Books, 1990), p. 151.
2. A story told by Diane Dreher in *The Tao of Personal Leadership* (New York: Harper Collins, 1996), p. 20.
3. Eleanor Clift, "Schroeder's Last Stand," *Working Woman,* April 1996, pp. 44–46.
4. Aldous Huxley, "Visionary Experience," in *The Highest State of Consciousness,* ed. John White (New York: Archer, 1972), as discussed in Robert Kegan's *The Evolving Self* (Cambridge, Mass.: Harvard University Press, 1983), p. 11.

Chapter One: The Family Template: Transforming the Influence of Family

1. Jerome Bruner, *In Search of Mind* (New York: Harper and Row, 1983), p. 3.
2. James Hillman, *The Soul's Code* (New York: Warner Books, 1997), pp. 63–91.
3. An additional source about Zion Preparatory Academy includes Dori Jones Jang, "Lots of Love and No Excuses," *Business Week,* 8 May 1995, p. 28.
4. Steven Chin, "Shelter Director: Artists in Action," *San Francisco Examiner,* 29 May 1994, p. B-3.
5. Additional sources for John Mackey's profile include Charles Fishman, "Good Teams, Fast Company," pp. 103–110; and Nick Patoski, "Winning the Food Fight," *Texas Monthly,* September 1996, pp. 119–21.

6. An additional source for Gene Silberberg's profile was Marcia Coburn, "Strong Suits," *Chicago,* June 1996, pp. 66–69.

7. For the parents-don't-matter paradigm, consult Judith Harris, *The Nurture Assumption* (New York: Free Press, 1998).

Chapter Two: The World as Teacher: Learning from Exemplars and Experience

1. This point is inspired by a discussion in James Loder, *The Transforming Moment* (Colorado Springs: Helmers and Howard, 1989), pp. 51–52.

2. John Gardner, *Leading Minds* (New York: Basic Books, 1995), pp. 41–65.

3. Additional sources for Tim Girvin's profile include Debra Prinzing, "Tim Girvin Design," *HOW Magazine,* December 1997; and Carol Smith, "Designer's Success a Sum of All Parts," *Seattle Post-Intelligencer,* 28 March 1997, p. B-1.

4. James Hillman, *The Soul's Code* (New York: Warner Books, 1997) p. 76.

5. The use of the term *exemplar* was suggested by discussions in Daniel Levinson, *The Seasons of a Man's Life* (New York: Ballantine Books, 1978); and Howard Gardner, *Extraordinary Minds* (New York: Basic Books, 1997), pp. 110–13, 116.

6. Antoine de Saint-Exupéry, *The Little Prince* (New York: Harcourt Brace, 1943), p. 85.

7. See Hillman, *The Soul's Code,* pp. 113–27, for a rich discussion of the blessing of being "perceived." Also see Linda Phillips, *Mentors and Protégées* (New York: Arbor House, 1982), for the crucial blessing of a "mentor prototype."

8. An additional source for Stephen Cannell's profile includes Andy Meisler, "High Flyer: From *Rockford* to Profit, Stephen J. Cannell Follows His Creative Instincts," *New York Times,* 28 April 1997.

9. In his extraordinary book *Revolution of the Heart* (New York: Riverhead Books, 1995), Bill Shore talks about a number of lessons in leadership.

10. Margo Murray, *Beyond the Myths and Magic of Mentoring* (San Francisco: Jossey Bass, 1991), p. 7; and Phillips, *Mentors and Protégées.*

11. See Levinson, *The Seasons of a Man's Life,* p. 101.

Chapter Three: The Moments of Meaning: Translating Events into Commitments

1. The discussion of moments of meaning is an adaptation of a key element in the provocative work of Robert Kegan, especially as detailed in *The Evolving Self.* Harvard University Press, 1983.

2. James Loder, *The Transforming Moment* (Colorado Springs: Hemers and Howard, 1989), p. 33.

3. Herbert Fingarette, *The Self in Transformation* (New York: Harper and Row, 1963), pp. 62–68.

4. A point made by Robert Kegan in lecturing at the Harvard Graduate School of Education in 1973.

5. Arthur Koestler, *The Act of Creation* (New York: Macmillan, 1964), pp. 35, 178–179.

6. Loder, *The Transforming Moment,* p. 4.

7. Additional sources for Scott Oki's profile include Adam Kleiner, "Scott Oki, Inc.," *Washington CEO,* May 1996, pp. 13–17; and Todd Jones, "A Passion for Giving," *Costco Connection,* May 1997, pp. 34–36.

8. Lillian Hellman, *Pentimento* (New York: Little Brown, 1973), p. 3.

Chapter Four: Reflection: Examining Experience

1. Additional sources for Harold Shapiro's profile include Ann Waldron, "The Ties That Bind," *Princeton Alumni Weekly,* January 1993, 17–23; and J. I. Marritt, "Steady as She Goes," *Princeton Alumni Weekly,* spring 1995, pp. 10–16.

2. Caroline Moseley, "What Is College For?" *Princeton Weekly Bulletin,* 21 March 1994.

3. See Howard Gardner, *Extraordinary Minds* (New York: Basic

Books, 1997), for an analysis of the dimensions of introspection, pp. 95–98, and reflection, pp. 146–47.

4. Additional sources for David Giuliani's profile include David Freedman, "Sonic Boom," *Inc. Magazine,* November 1997, pp. 38–42; and Monte Enbysk, "David Giuliani: Optiva's Low Key CEO," *Washington CEO,* March 1998, pp. 21–24.

5. Stephen Glenn and Jane Nelsen discuss this distinct process of perception in their book, *Raising Self-Reliant Children in a Self-Indulgent World* (Rocklin: Prima Publishing, 1989), pp. 51–56.

6. Daniel Coleman, *Emotional Intelligence* (New York: Bantam Books, 1995), pp. 41–46.

7. See, for example, D. H. Lawrence, "New Heaven and Earth," in *D. H. Lawrence,* ed. Vivian Sola Pinto and Warren Roberts (New York: Viking Press, 1964), pp. 256–60.

8. Additional sources for Ellen Futter's profile include James Traub, "Shake Them Bones," *New Yorker,* 13 March 1995; and Glenn Collins, "Museum of Natural History Welcomes Its New President," *New York Times,* 2 December 1993.

9. J. D. Salinger, "Catcher in the Rye," as quoted in Traub, "Shake Them Bones," p. 48.

10. Additional sources for John Bryan's profile include Judith Crown, "Bryan Knits Global Vision, Local Action," *Crain's: Chicago Business,* 15 June 1992; and "Bryan Experiences Key to Business Strategy," *USA Today,* 27 April 1998, p. B8.

11. Herbert Fingarette, *The Self in Transformation* (New York: Harper and Row, 1963), p. 20.

Chapter Five: Framework: Creating an Optimistic Narrative

1. An additional source was Wilma Mankiller and Michael Wallis, *Mankiller: A Chief and Her People* (New York: St. Martin's Press, 1993).

2. Martin A. Seligman, *The Optimistic Child* (Boston: Houghton Mifflin, 1995), p. 52.

3. Herbert Fingarette, *The Self in Transformation* (New York: Harper and Row, 1963), pp. 22–23.

4. An additional source was Brenda Lauderback, "Someone Said You Can't," *Executive Female*, July–August 1997.

5. Kegan, *The Evolving Self* (Cambridge: Harvard University Press, 1983), pp. 2–3.

6. Bill Shore, *Revolution of the Heart* (New York: Riverhead Books, 1995), pp. 21–36.

7. Martin Seligman, *Learned Optimism* (New York: Pocket Books, 1990), p. 151.

8. Ibid., p. 19.

9. Ibid., p. 20.

10. An additional source for Phyllis Campbell's profile was Doree Rae Armstrong, "Phyllis Campbell: Holding the Door Open for Others to Follow," *Destination Issaquah*, winter 1997.

11. John Stanford's life and work have been widely reported in a number of sources, including Steven Goldsmith, "A Force for Children," *Seattle Post-Intelligencer*, 30 November 1998.

12. Personal communication with Roger Erskine on 16 December 1998.

13. Sources about John Stanford's illness and memorial service include Ruth Teichroeb and John Iwasaki, "Stanford's Legacy: Hope," *Seattle Post-Intelligencer*, 3 December 1998; and Dick Mallory, "Don't Ever Give Up," *Virginia Mason Magazine*, summer 1998, pp. 4–7.

14. e. e. cummings, "Love Is a Place," in *No Thanks* (New York: Liveright, 1978), p. 58.

Chapter Six: Attunement: Learning from Those You Lead

1. Additional sources for Mitchell Rabkin's profile include Alex Phas, "Human Touch at the Top," *Boston Globe*, 7 March 1995; D. C. Denison, "The Interview: Mitchell Rabkin," *Boston Globe*, summer 1997; and Robert Rosen, *Leading with People* (New York: Viking, 1996), pp. 273–80.

2. Additional sources for Shelly Lazarus include Stuart Elliot, "From One Woman to Another," *New York Times*, 9 September

1996; and Lacia Bird, "Lazarus IBM Coup Was All about Relationships," *Wall Street Journal,* 26 May 1994.

3. An additional source for Carolyn McKecuen's profile includes Anne Lowrey Bailey, "An Economic Savior for Rural Women," *The Chronicle of Philanthropy* 4, no. 18 (1994).

4. George Kelley, *A Theory of Personality: The Psychology of Personal Constructs* (New York: WW Norton, 1963).

5. Robert Kegan, *The Evolving Self* (Cambridge, Mass.: Harvard University Press, 1983), pp. 32–33, 36–39.

6. Ibid., pp. 41–45.

7. Edmund Husserl and Donn Welton *The Essential Husserl* (Bloomington: Indiana University Press, 1999).

Chapter Seven: Conviction: Relying on Inner Authority

1. Additional sources for Fred Rogers's profile include Jeanne Marie Laskas, "The Good Life and Work of Mister Rogers," *Life Magazine,* June 1994; David Rensin, "The Last Safe Neighborhood," *TV Guide,* 7 March 1992, pp. 24–25; John Sedwig, "Welcome to Mister Rogers' Neighborhood," *Wigwag Magazine;* and Tom Junod, "Can You Say Hero?" *Esquire,* November 1998, p. 132.

2. This idea of speaking from experience is central to Elizabeth Debold, Marie Wilson, and Idelisse Malave, *Mother Daughter Revolution* (New York: Addison Wesley, 1993); and Lyn Mikel Brown and Carol Gilligan, *Meeting at the Crossroads* (New York: Ballantine Books, 1992).

3. Laskas, "The Good Life and Work of Mr. Rogers," pp. 72–76.

4. Junod, "Can You Say Hero?" p. 138.

5. Debold, Wilson, and Malave, *Mother Daughter Revolution,* p. 129. The notion of becoming author to one's own experience also appears in the work of Søren Kierkegaard, *Fear and Trembling* (New York: Penguin, 1986).

6. Additional sources of Leroy Hood's profile include Laurie Garrett, "Mapping the Human Genetic Code," *Los Angeles Times Magazine,* 3 March 1996; Kate Ledger, "Superstar Scientist,"

Hopkins Medical News, winter 1996, pp. 31–35; and Ed Regis, "Hacking the Mother Code," *Wired,* September 1995, p. 137.

7. Willis, Tom, Justin and Michael Toms, *True Work* (New York: Bell Tower, 1998).

8. Additional sources for Ed Lewis's profile include Lorraine Calvacca, "The Lewis Expedition," *Folio,* May 1956, pp. 46–47; and Mary Huhn, "The Essential Publisher," *New York Post,* 2 November 1997.

9. Prescott Lecky, *Self-Consistency: A Theory of Personality* (Fort Meyers, Fla.: Island Press, 1945), pp. 109–13.

10. John Clemons and Douglas Mayer, *The Classic Touch: Lessons in Leadership from Homer to Hemingway* (Homewood: DowJones Irwin, 1987) pp. 50–58.

11. Additional sources for Dave Duffield's profile include Bruce Upbin, "Have Fun, Kill the Enemy," *Forbes* (1997); Doug Bartholomew, "Successful? Try, Try Again," *Industry Week,* 2 February 1998; and Adrienne Fox, "PeopleSoft's Dave Duffield: How a Techie Became Known for Great Customer Service," *Investors Business Daily,* 3 April 1998.

12. A fascinating description of Pericles' creation and Athenian "corporate culture" appears in John Clemons and Douglas Mayer, *The Classic Touch: Lessons in Leadership from Homer to Hemingway* (Homewood: DowJones Irwin, 1987), pp. 51–56.

13. An additional source for Francesca Zambello's profile includes Terry Teachout, "Rattling the Cage," *Time,* 3 August 1998.

14. Additional sources for Paul Wellstone's profile include Jim Ragsdales and Bill Salisbury, "Trading Places," *St. Paul Pioneer Press,* 6 October 1966; and E. J. Dionne, "Not Quite Your Typical Radical," *Washington Post Magazine,* 19 January 1997.

15. Mary McGrory, "Virtuously, Minnesota," *Washington Post,* 8 December 1996.

16. Clemons and Mayer, *The Classic Touch,* pp. 108–9.

17. Harold Bloom, *Shakespeare and the Invention of the Human* (New York: Putnam, 1998), pp. 409–11.

18. William Shakespeare, *The Tragedy of Hamlet, Prince of Denmark,* ed. Barnett Sylvan (New York: Signet, 1998), p. 22.

Chapter Eight: Replenishment: Restoring Perspective

1. Additional sources for John Bryan's profile include Judith Dobrzynski, "Sara Lee Is Donating Its Impressionist Art to Museums," *New York Times,* 3 June 1998, p. B-1; and John Kimmelman, "Southern Comfort," *Financial World,* 4 January 1994.
2. Michael Gelb, *How to Think Like Leonardo da Vinci* (New York: Delacorte, 1998), p. 158.
3. Ibid., p. 159.
4. An additional source for Beckie Masaki's profile includes Steven Chin, "Shelter Director: Artist in Action," *San Francisco Examiner,* 29 May 1994, p. B-3.
5. An additional source for Phyllis Campbell's profile includes Hugh Kugiya, "Banking on Kindness," *Seattle Times Magazine,* 2 June 1996.

Endnote: Leadership as a Habit of Mind

1. Additional sources for Ruth Simmons's profile include *Current Biography,* January 1996, pp. 44–48; and B. J. Roche, "Making History," *Boston Globe Magazine,* September 1995.
2. Alfred Adler's work is described in H. L. Ansbacher and R. R. Ansbacher, *The Individual Psychology of Alfred Adler* (New York: Basic Books, 1956); and Rudolph Kurs and Loren Grey, *Logical Consequences: The New Approach to Discipline* (New York: Penguin Books, 1968).
3. Personal communication, July 1998.

Appendixes

Appendix A: Authors' Note

The focus of the book's research, as gathered through the "Inner Work Interviews," was to create a connection between a leader's past and present. The central question: How does a leader's legacy—the relationships and experiences in a leader's past—influence his or her experience of meeting the challenges of being in charge?

To answer this question, we interviewed sixty-five leaders who, in addition to being widely recognized for their success in leading a profitable and/or purposeful organization, were identified as thoughtful, insightful, and articulate about their experiences as a leader. They are listed in Appendix B. A number of interview subjects were leaders with whom we had a professional relationship. Others were selected through suggestions from our colleagues, referrals from interviewees, and media profiles. A deliberate choice was made to vary geography, organizational mission, ethnicity, and sex among interview subjects.

The earliest interviews concentrated on exploring how three aspects of a leader's legacy (family, exemplars, and life-changing experiences) had influenced how leaders think about, and react to, complex and challenging situations in their day-to-day leadership.

Early in the data collection, a dominant pattern emerged. Clearly, leaders who had created meaning, and learned from, the events and relationships of their lifetime had translated that meaning into several consistent thought patterns. These habits of mind included reflection, framework, attunement, conviction, and—with less frequency—replenishment.

As the research progressed, interviews were equally weighted between questions about legacy and those about the habits of mind identified. Each interview included selected questions drawn from the questionnaire in Appendix C.

Although we interviewed sixty-five leaders, and gained insight from each one, we were not able to include data from all of the interviews in the book. Instead, we selected the stories that most clearly illustrated aspects of legacy and habits of mind.

Appendix B

People Interviewed for this Book*

Neil Austrian, president and COO, National Football League
Barbara Atkinson, dean, Allegheny School of Medicine
Anat Bird, COO, Roosevelt Bank, St. Louis
Cathleen Black, president, Hearst Magazines
Barbara Davis Blum, Chairman, President, and CEO, Adams
    National Bank
Neil Braun, president, NBC Television
Ellen Bravo, codirector, 9to5, National Association of Working
    Women
John Bryan, chairman and CEO, Sara Lee
Phyllis Campbell, president, U.S. Bank of Washington
Stephen J. Cannell, chairman, Cannell Studios
Candace Carpenter, CEO, iVillage.com
Gun Denhart, Chair and cofounder, Hanna Andersson
Nancy Dickey, chairperson, American Medical Association
Dave Duffield, chairman, CEO, and president, PeopleSoft
Ellen Futter, president, American Museum of Natural History, New
    York
Patricia Gallup, cofounder, chairman, and CEO, PC Connection
Al Gamper, chairman, CEO, and president, CIT Financial Group
Tim Girvin, CEO, Tim Girvin Design
David Giuliani, CEO, Optiva Corporation
Ellen Gordon, president, COO, Tootsie Roll Industries
Gerald Grinstein, former chairman, CEO, Burlington Northern
Bruce Hallett, President, Time, Inc.

*Some of the indiviudals interviewed are not mentioned by name in this book.
Those whose names are included can be found in the index.

Leroy Hood, Ph.D., chairman, Department of Molecular
    Biotechnology, University of Washington
Harvey Jones, chairman and CEO, Cutter and Buck, Inc.
Harry Kamen, chairman of the board and CEO, Metropolitan Life
Joanna Lau, chairman, Lau Technologies
Brenda Lauderback, president, Retail Group, Nine West
Shelly Lazarus, chairman and CEO, Ogilviy & Mather
Ed Lewis, chairman and CEO, Essence Communications
Gary Locke, governor, State of Washington
George Lynn, president and CEO, AtlantiCare
John Mackey, founder and CEO, Whole Foods
Andy MacPhail, president, Chicago Cubs
Chief Wilma Mankiller, former chief, Cherokee Nation
Beckie Masaki, executive director, Asian Women's Shelter, San
    Francisco
William Mays, president, Mays Chemical Company
Carolyn McKecuen, founder and executive director, Watermark
    Association of Artisans
Stanley O. McNaughton, CEO, PEMCO Financial Services
Rich Mellman, CEO, Lettuce Entertain You, Inc.
Scott Oki, chairman, Oki Foundation
J'Amy Owen, president, The Retail Group
Mitchell Rabkin, M.D., CEO, Care Group, Harvard Teaching Hospital
    of Beth Israel
Brigadier General Karen Rankin, United States Air Force
Edward Rendell, mayor, Philadelphia
Gary Reikes, president, The Reikes Institute
Leonard Riggio, CEO, Barnes & Noble
Fred Rogers, executive producer, *Mister Rogers' Neighborhood,* and
    CEO, Family Communications
Elaine Rosen, president, UNUM America
Sallie Rowland, chairman and CEO of Rowland Designs
Patricia Schroeder, former congresswoman, State of Colorado, and
    president, Association of American Publishers
Gerard Schwarz, music director, Seattle Symphony Orchestra
Harold Shapiro, president, Princeton University

Bill Shore, executive director, Share Our Strength
Gene Silberberg, president, Bigsby & Kruthers
Ruth Simmons, president, Smith College
Jim Sinegal, CEO, Costco
John Stanford, superintendent of Seattle Public Schools, Seattle
Al Steffans, CEO, Stratos Product Development, Inc.
Daniel Sullivan, Broadway and film director, *The Heidi Chronicles, The Dinner Party,* and other plays
Rick Swig, president, RSBA & Associates
Esther Torres, founder of the Community Development Corporation, and president, Torres & Associates
Burton Visotsky, rabbi, Jewish Theological Seminary, New York
Janice Weinman, executive director, American Association of University Women
Paul Wellstone, senator, State of Minnesota
Doug Wheeler, principal, Zion Preparatory Academy, Seattle
Francesca Zambello, director, international opera

Appendix C: The Inner Work Interview

Inner Resources

- We often hear that exceptional leaders draw upon inner resources to make tough decisions and face the challenges of being in charge. When you find yourself in a particularly difficult situation, what are the resources within yourself that are a source of strength for you?

Family Template: How do leaders demonstrate the lessons from childhood in their leadership?

- Describe each of your parents during your childhood years. What lessons (both positive and negative) learned from them are reflected in the way you lead your organization? Other adults?
- Who were the leaders in your family? Which qualities of their leadership have influenced you?
- Give me an example of a family event, milestone, or loss that touched everyone in your family.
- Tell me a story that suggests the role you played in your family.

Exemplars: How do leaders incorporate lessons from the people who have influenced them in their leadership?

- In looking back, was the leader in you already evident as a child? Tell me about a time when you first demonstrated your ability to take charge.

- Tell me about someone who was a hero/heroine for you when you were growing up. What lessons from them do you bring to your role as a leader?

- Who are the three people who had the most impact on your approach to leadership? What positive or negative lessons did you learn from them?

The interview included *selected* questions draw from this questionnaire.

- Leaders often talk about someone outside the family who discovered them—in early life, a teacher or coach; in later years, a boss. Was there someone who "discovered" you, gave you a chance to lead?

Reflection or Illuminating Moments: How do leaders reflect about their experiences and learn from them?

- Leaders often talk about experiences they view as life changing—illuminating moments that shift their values and perspective. Tell me a story about such a time in your life.

- Tell me a story about an experience that stretched you personally and deepened your experience or insights about being in charge. Can you think of an experience that changed your style of leadership or allowed you to reinvent yourself?

- We find that exceptional leaders have the ability to see events in context—in light of the bigger picture. Can you tell me how this works for you? Can you think of a time when in the midst of a crisis you stood back and gained the larger perspective that helped you cope with the event?

- We find that strong leaders have the capacity to observe themselves—to understand how others see them. How would you describe the way you go about appraising your own behavior and gauging the impact you have on the people you lead?

Conviction: How do leaders develop a strong value system and find purpose in their work?

- Give me an example about how a value you learned from a parent, teacher, or mentor is expressed in your work.
- When I ask, What do you find most meaningful about your work and what gives you a sense of purpose as a leader? what comes to mind?
- Tell me a story about a time when your values shaped a specific decision in your organization.

Framework: How do leaders explain adversity or interpret their mistakes?

- Tell me a story about a time you faced a major disappointment or made a significant mistake or error in judgment. Do you recall your thoughts when you first realized the problem? How did you "explain" the situation to yourself?
- Do you ever use humor to soften the blow of stressful situations?
- Recall a time in your career as a leader when you faced a particularly challenging situation or just plain bad luck. What did you learn from surviving the situation?
- We find that many leaders have optimistic habits of mind (their way of explaining negative events allows them to cope even amid a crisis). How would you describe your typical thought process when faced with a crisis?
- Have you had to confront significant losses or major disappointments in your work or home life? What resources helped

you through this experience? How did this experience contribute to your perspective as a leader?

- Give me an example of a time when you made an error in
  judgment or failed in pursuit of a goal. How did you bounce
  back from the experience?
- When you think back to parents, teachers, or mentors, can
  you think of anyone who influenced the way you "think your
  way through" a crisis?

Attunement: How do leaders deal with the isolation of being in charge and learn from the people they lead?

- Tell me about a time when you felt most alone in your role as
  a leader.
- How did you cope and get support?
- We always hear, "It's lonely at the top." What comes to mind?
- How do you deal day-to-day with the isolation of being a
  leader?
- Being a leader is a heady experience. How do you maintain a
  sense of humility and proportion?
- Being responsible for an organization can be a distancing experience. Tell me a story about a time when your authority
  kept you from understanding what others in your organization were thinking or feeling.
- How do you gain an understanding of the people you lead
  and put yourself in their shoes?

Inner Authority: How do leaders follow their own point of view—to trust their judgment when taking risks or making decisions?

- Being in charge requires that you trust your own judgment—
  even when others don't agree. Can you think of a time when

you stood alone in making a decision you believed in? How did you find the resolve to persist in your point of view?

- Was there ever a time in your career when family or a valued adviser doubted your course or decision? What strengthened you to persist?

- Tell me about a time when you faced a challenge where no one could really help you. What allowed you to confront the challenge on your own?

Replenishment: How do leaders manage time away from work wisely, so it is restorative and reinvigorates their job performance?

- Being in charge can be a setup for not spending enough time with family. How have you dealt with this challenge?

- List some ways that you use time away from work for self-renewal, so it is restorative and reinvigorating.

- So many people know who you are. Tell me a story about a time when this interfered with your life outside the office. How do you protect your privacy?

Index